Gem of a Soul

A GUIDE TO REBOOTING YOUR MIND

AND BEING YOUR BEST VERSION

VISHAL KUMAR

ISBN 979-8-88733-624-4

Dedicated to all humble humans who wish to shed the status-quo and embrace the path of Growth and Inspiration.

Join me in making this world a better place!

I HAVE A DREAM.........

\# I have a dream. A hopeful dream that every leader at every walk of life shall realise that his worth is not so much to do with his **competence** as it is to do with his *ability to **inspire** & lead from front* and have a **character** *that's world class.*

\# I have a dream. An achievable dream that one day, the world will be richly populated with souls whose dictum is founded on **selfless service** & not on **selfish selling**.

\# I have a dream. A wishful dream that we humans will one day, stop attaching a person's **net-worth** with his **self-worth**.

\# I have a dream. A palpable dream that every human alive on this planet earth will realise that *the only **competition is with self*** & that being the **best version of self** is the greatest achievement; with an everlasting inspiration and belief that the **Best is yet to come**.

\# I have a dream. A longing dream that **religion & politics** *shall no longer be the reason for conflicts between people and nations*; And that the world shall soon come to terms with the only religion that can ever serve us well till eternity – **Humility in Humanity**.

\# I have a dream. A fairy-tale dream that all organisations with hierarchical set ups will one day realise that it's the **world-class organisational climate** that dictates the output & not the dictatorial leaders who profess **carrot & stick**; And that every organisation will be a team whose members won't desperately long for holidays.

\# I have a dream. A world-changing dream that one day, no human, howsoever ordinary, shall be fearful or anxious of having an **extraordinary dream or vision** for the world today is literally moved by those ordinary men & women who dared to dream.

I have a dream. And you should have one too! for the world today needs ordinary men & women who dare to dream.......

But it's not enough to dream. A dream without a plan is just a wish. Hence, I have a plan too – encapsulated in this book to serve you to lead lives that are inspiring and impactful. Join me in this soul-searching joy ride.

CONTENTS

Part II Deconstruct True Leadership

Part III Fuel Your Growth

PRELUDE

<table><tr><td>1</td><td>

WHY I BEGAN (AND WHY YOU CAN TOO)...

</td></tr></table>

Every mission has a cause. So has mine. Allow me to quickly share why I actually took to writing a book. To be very honest, writing a book was never on my mind, especially, given the nature of my profession. However, certain unusually overwhelming events have unfolded in the last three years that have suddenly put me into a different orbit.

It all began when, back in September 2019, I decided to recalibrate and take charge of how my day unfolded and thus joined the clan of early risers (of course inspired from *The 5 AM Club* by Robin Sharma and also '*The Miracle Morning*' by Hal Elrod). As clichéd as it may seem, I was intrigued by the concept of Kick-Starting each day with something positive as I wake up. As social media is the only place where you can share your thoughts with the world while retaining the liberty of revisiting them the whole day, I began posting inspiring quotes and photos as status on WhatsApp every morning. At times, I even posted extracts of inspirational books with highlighted text with a genuine intent of spreading positive vibes each day.

As days passed by, I was flooded with a flurry of positive responses from all and sundry in my phonebook including my classmates, teachers, colleagues, subordinates and even seniors. Some even took the liberty of taking screenshots and storing them in their phones while a few others simply reposted it as their status. There were even days on which I was super-busy to post anything on WhatsApp and many even pinged me to check out if I am OK. And that was really a needle mover for me. I was amazed by how little it takes to uplift spirits of all those around you and how even a mediocre mind like me might strike a chord with even the A-Players if the thoughts are founded on the right principles. That was the point I decided to make it big. Not for me, not for money and not for fame but for the sole purpose of spreading positivity and inspiration to as many people as possible on this planet and not just my phonebook! This is also the very reason why, though, it's my first book, I am sanguine it won't fall on deaf ears or strike blind eyes. The greatest achievement for any author is to enable his or her readers to relate the contents effortlessly to their lives – personal and professional alike. While I am conscious of carrying that burden, I am also convinced that it will touch your heart and soul.

My Credentials

I won't be surprised if the environment makes a decision of reading this book purely based on my credentials. Yes, that's how we operate in everything we do and choose isn't it? While choosing a book, we choose a *'Bestseller'*, while choosing a girlfriend, we want the *hottest chick in the town*, while investing, we choose the one which has a reputation of *guaranteed returns* and while choosing a movie to watch, we see the *IMDB* and the *reputation of the artists and directors* straight away. So, it might just disappoint you to learn that I ain't a bigshot! I am just a plain and simple solider of the Indian Army who is making a genuine attempt of injecting that everlasting inspiration into anyone who lays hands on this book so that you never feel disheartened or disgruntled at your workplaces or home fronts. I can however take a little credit to have taken a pause in this jet paced rat-race and retrospected on the worthiness of it all. Having spent more than 20 years in the environs of *Discipline, Honesty, Integrity, Values* and unquestionable *Obedience*, one thing that has stuck with me and etched in my grey matter like a tattoo is this – **'If a human being, having been blessed to stand apart amongst all the creatures on planet earth, can't inspire those around him or her by their mere presence, uplift them to realise their potential and make them smile and motivated, what good is it to live at all?'**.

My Target Audience

If you have reached this far without lamenting on why you chose to read this book, congratulations! You are exactly the kind of audience I am genuinely interested in making an impact on. This book is for those who have decided to take a leap from being **'Victims'** to being **'Victors'**. It's all about how just by fixing who you are, you fix the whole world around you. It has taken years of research and deep thinking to handcraft this book as I wanted it to perfectly coincide with my deepest values and beliefs. All I can say with utmost humility and faith is that once you have flipped through the last page, you will thank god that it happened to you! So, I guess we are now ready to take a plunge and make a Giant Leap! Let's begin....

How to go About this Book

This book isn't the one to be hurried off and shelved. I urge you to go ultra-slow in browsing through it. Make notes, highlight the important contents which you feel have touched you. I won't be dejected at all if you take months to wrap it up as that's exactly what I intend. I have carved this book in a manner that it acts as your moral and inspirational compass whenever you feel deserted physically and mentally and promises to give you that *'Feel-Good Factor'* everytime you revisit its contents. I am in no hurry of getting your feedbacks or making it to some bestseller list. So, be slow and digest it in entirety. Who knows, this might just end up being a life changer for you!

2   THE LOGICAL GROWTH MODEL OF AN IMPACTFUL LEADER

All humans desirous of making an impact in this world or to their society, so to speak, have an innate desire for self-growth because deep down we do realise that charity begins at home, don't we? But there is a big difference between wanting something and knowing how to get it! I am reminded of one of my teachers during my school days who always urged us to make a plan for whatever our goals are because, she said, **'An aim without a plan is just a wish'** and not all wishes come true unless you get on to the ground and soil your hands and thus cleanse your soul. Each one of us wants to have a good career, a voluminous bank balance and an enjoyable life but few are willing to take that less traversed path full of slogging and hustle that enables us manifest our unique dreams into reality. And I bet my last ten bucks, it isn't all that hunky-dory. You may ask any human on this planet earth who has achieved great things, be it a sportsperson, an artist, a business tycoon or military folks about how they feel to have come this far which, for most humans, remains only a distant dream. Sure, they will tell you they feel happy and satisfied but you won't ever see them all super-excited about it because, hands on heart, they do realise how painful and unapologetic their journey was, trudging past some of the most gruelling and testing times any person wanting to make a mark would have to embrace and withstand. You always remember your struggles but all those around you always remember your achievements. Talk about perspective.

Back to manifesting your innate desires, if you want to embrace growth in all dimensions of your life and NOT just restrict it your Jobs/Professions that puts bread on your plates, Good News! You have laid your hands on just the right kind of book. Honestly, I am not a big fan of '3 Step Success Formula' kind of stuff because I firmly believe there are as many formulae as there are 'conscious human minds' working to resolve a problem and the methodology of 'One Size Fits All' is absurd to say the least. Yet, may I humbly suggest, the process of Growth in itself has certain inherent processes which are inevitable and without which your ascendancy may not be permanent. In other words, they are non-negotiable for a realistic growth. Hence, I am tempted to refer to it as a *Logical Growth Model* for any human being who strives to make a mark and make a difference. Please have a look at the model below.

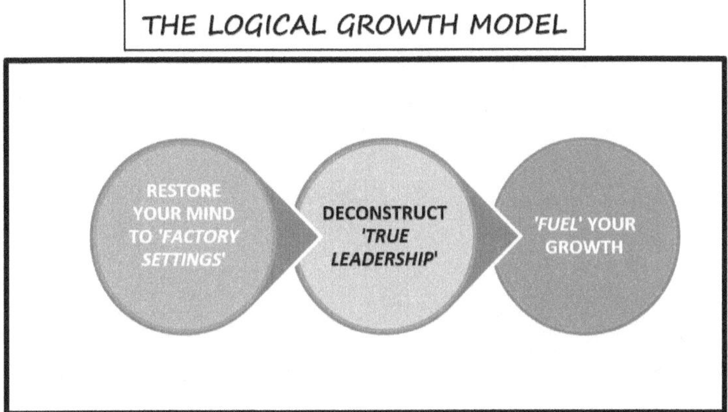

The aforesaid sequence is of importance because one must precede and lead to the other in the same order to have a lasting impact and how! I shall dig deep into each of these processes as we venture out together through this book and acquaint you with all that it takes to realise growth in your professional and personal lives which, If I may suggest, isn't exactly bi-dimensional as most of us perceive.

PART I

RESTORE YOUR MIND TO FACTORY SETTINGS

3 WHY RESTORE?

> "No one is born hating another person because of colour of his skin or background or his religion. People must learn to hate, and if they can learn to hate, they can be taught to love, for love comes more naturally to human heart than its opposite".
>
> – *Nelson Mandela*

I know what comes to your mind when you read the title of part I of this book. We do the same to our smartphones when they get uncomfortably corrupted don't we?

This is based on the thematic premise that the factory settings of a mobile phone are best suited for its optimal functioning barring a few security related fixes which are tailor-made for specific users.

Equate the mobile phone to your body and the settings to your *Beliefs and Mindset*. Whatever may be your age today, ever since our births, your *mind* has interacted with millions of souls, spent time at plethora of places and experienced zillion things. Yet each one of them has had some impact on our beliefs and mindsets and the way we perceive things. Just to quote a plain instance – my cousin was a hard core non-vegetarian until one day her father took her to the place where it all manifests, the meat shop! There was a sudden sub-conscious rush of compassion and kindness in her, as she narrated later, which drove her to go vegan for life! Sounds familiar, isn't it?

That is not to say or profess that eating meat is unethical or bad. The point I am trying to make is simply this – We are all born with Factory (read default) Settings but the notion of practicality of this real world fed to us by the society makes it go haywire. So much so that we are no longer the person we were in terms of beliefs a decade ago. Similar analogy could be drawn about kindness and helpfulness. Go to a random kid feeding off his/her lunch box at a school and plead for some. The kid will offer you without blinking an eye! The same kid however grows up to become more practical, transactional and competitive by interacting with the so-called real world. Let's broaden the scope now to *Lying, Cheating, Stealing* and other tools of unethical pursuits. Was any child born with these traits? I bet you not. Consider these -

> # **Love** is natural, **Hatred** is taught.

> # **Unconditional help** is natural, **Transactional Attitude** is taught.

> # **Authenticity** is natural, **Fakery** is taught.

> # **Truthfulness** is natural, **Manipulation** is taught.

> # **Genuine happiness for others** is Natural, **Jealousy** is taught.

> # **Honesty** is natural, **Crookedness** is taught.

> # **Calmness** is natural, **Anger** is taught.

> # **Humility** is natural, **Arrogance** and **Inflated Ego** is taught.

> # **Giving** is natural, **Taking** is taught.

> # **Being an Asset** is natural, **Being a Parasite** is taught.

> # **Pro-activeness** is natural, **Procrastination** is taught.

But who teaches them? Us and the society by the way we deal with authenticity shown by people! Consider these simple instances – Most bosses so bonkers at you when you say, *'Sorry I forgot'*. Most parents will slap their kids if, say, they confide in them about *Smoking* or *Stealing*. **The more we disrespect authenticity through our response, more fakery is being generated which is permanent**. Ironically though, people adore Authenticity and not Fakery. Well, it's not just about resetting our fundamentals like Honesty, Integrity, Kindness and Compassion. There are are a lot more that are less talked of but more urgent than ever if you truly want to *'Bloom where you're Planted'* and inspire all around you to be their Best Versions. Restoring our minds to factory settings is a precursor to begin with, and a catalyst thereafter, to being authentic, to appreciate authenticity and weed out fakery from this world. And the first baby step towards this restoration is understanding the importance of the most underrated emotion in my opinion called the *Gratitude*. And that's where we tee-off.

4 'MY CUP RUNNETH OVER'

"Thou preparest a table before me in the presence of mine enemies: thou anointest my head with oil; my cup runneth over".

– Psalm 23:5

Most of us are predators of precious time. I say this after a lot of forethought because we waste too much of time in lamenting over what we don't have or haven't accomplished. We are dead-attached to the *'Glorified Ends'* disregarding the beautiful journey in the process. **We are anxious and excited about what's cooking in the *'Kitchen of Fate'* than what our deeds have offered on our plate**. Let us ask ourselves a simple question – How many of us take time to express Gratitude for whatever we already have? Acquainting you all with the perils of not being grateful for 'What's on Your Plate Today' is the burden of this chapter. If you even have an iota of belief in higher powers or almighty or God in any form; if you have ever whispered Thank God or Oh God or God Bless, my analogy will make lot of sense.

Imagine you have a friend who is in trouble and has sought your help. You being a humble human, bail him/her out. And guess what! That person couldn't care less about thanking you. While you may ignore the same being a one-time aberration, if that person repeatedly does that to you, would you be equally motivated to help him/her again and again? This is Your Truth Serum! Thankless people don't inspire anyone on this globe.

Having said that, aren't we manifesting ourselves into 'thankless of sorts' by not being grateful for what we already have? This is perhaps the closest analogy I could find as to why expressing Gratitude is so very important in our lives. **Gratitude weeds out greed and harvests prosperity to unimaginable levels**.

This by no means suggests that you use Gratitude as a sledgehammer to kill your ambitions and dreams of getting a notch higher. It only means you begin your hustle each day with a mindset that you have enough and use it as a fuel to propel your efforts to achieve more. You will come back each day happy and satisfied irrespective of the result.

In my humble view, *if you are born in a humble family and are born with no physical deformities, if your parents offered you good education and your family has your back financially and emotionally, you already belong to the privileged section of the global populace. That doesn't at all mean being filthy rich, does it?* We must ask this to ourselves every single day to realise how gifted we are and vow not to let it go waste.

When we don't practice gratitude, and feel grateful for what we already have, strangely enough, all our actions conspire to slip away whatever we already have. A quintessential testimony is offered by singer Rihanna who indiscriminately spent all her money on *flashy in-things* only to find herself at the precipice of bankruptcy. Her financial advisor couldn't have said it better when he was sued by her – *"Was it necessary to tell her that if you spend money on things, you will end up with things and not money?"*

Take time to express Gratitude everyday. It could be through Journaling in a diary or by means of spoken words. Research shows that a mindset of Gratitude leaves no space for any other negative emotion to develop simultaneously. ***Instead of seeing the cup as half-empty or as half-full, let's always believe our cups are runneth over!*** We will now see the perils of not embracing the Attitude of Gratitude.

5 TOO MUCH OF 'NEVER SETTLE' CAN 'UNSETTLE' YOU FOREVER

A smartphone giant company has its tagline that reads '**Never Settle**'. Sure, it means we must be hungry for more and not stagnate in our quest for improvements and innovations. But what happens when we (like most today) don't calibrate these '*Urges to Inch Forward*'? We '**Unsettle Forever**'. Not staying satisfied or being grateful for what you're blessed with may at times shove us into a downward spiral. An interesting story to share which has my back.......

A certain Adeo Ressi of San Francisco was dejected and not satisfied with what he had accomplished in his life. Reason? He thought his college roommate had achieved way better than him. We will come back to his roommate later. First, let's get you wise with what this gentleman had achieved in his life thus far. *He started an entrepreneurial schooling firm called 'Founders Institute' at San Francisco which basically coached wanna be entrepreneurs to 'Learn it All' which went on to establish hundreds of schools (digital and physical) across 165 cities around the globe in multiple languages. As a consequence of his mentoring, as many as 2500 new start-ups and companies took birth.* Phew! But I said he wasn't happy, didn't I? He compared himself with his roommate who was....... none other than......*Elon Musk*! Talk about 'Never Settle'!

A man of his stature rather than building on his humungous feats only ended up comparing himself with another man (his roommate) who…. hold your breath….

Invented an Electric Car which was once considered Impossible

Built charging stations which was unconceivable

Made it cheaper than gasoline which was basically impossible

Built a rocket at 1/10th cost as that of NASA which was basically unconceivable

And then…Goodness gracious, he put a car on top of it and shot it up into space!

I heard one of my friends say '*Too much gratitude stagnates you*'. But what did too much 'Never Settle' kind of mindset do to Adeo Ressi or Many of us today! Getting a larger perspective on life's amazing gifts and its blessings on us is a fuel that drives a life full of gratitude. Feed your minds with '*countless thanks*' for the '*abundant blessings*' which, for many, is only a distant dream. Yet, many, like Adeo Ressi feed their grey matters with '*Overwhelming Feelings of Inadequacy*' and thus 'Never Settle' (read Unsettled Forever). And when you appreciate the adequacy, when your cup is runneth over, you physically and cognitively detach yourself from the illusionary pursuits and yet attract choicest of fortunes. We will see that in the next chapter.

6 THE POWER OF DETACHMENT

"The Law of Detachment says that in order to acquire anything in the physical universe, you have to relinquish your attachment to it".

– Deepak Chopra

Ask any athlete or a sportsman or a bodybuilder or a scientist involved in relentless research, what's one thing they have consistently focused on in their entire journey of life and you will hear an unanimous and an unambiguous answer – *Show up for practice every single day*. And that's all they aim the most. They aren't encumbered by the thoughts of winning or stresses of obstacles enroute. They are simply obsessed with showing up every day for the rest of their lives. In other words, they are ferociously attached with the process and dispassionately detached from the outcomes.

Ever since our childhoods, we have always been advised to have an aim or goal and chase it relentlessly with all madness and preparations. That we mustn't lose sight of our goal was a common punchline. Even Sun Tsu's Art of War postulates 'Selection and Maintenance of Aim' as a principle. *Yet, if there is one vital aspect of it all which most of us missed out on as children and even for majority of adulthood pursuits, it is this – Staying Committed to the Process that eventually ensures Success.* Thankfully, we now often hear many motivational speakers, eminent sports icons and coaches stressing on the

'**Process as a Vital Ingredient to Success**'. But that's only the '**What**' part of it. The '**How**' of it remains largely unanswered and unexplored and how!

Any goal or aim in our lives howsoever big or small can be further broken down into myriad processes as a recipe of sorts for the ultimate achievement. The hardest part, which you would agree, is sticking to the process or in other words *consistency. This applies to all and sundry – a primary school kid preparing for board exams or a teenager preparing for a competitive exam that supposedly will define his/her fate or a CEO/employee/leader of any organisation or any soul on this planet who wants to 'Achieve' and thereby be of 'Service' and 'Make an Impact' to the mankind.* Much strange as it may seem, the truth is, we can't just take our eyes of the '**Desired Glorious End State**'. And no surprises, we don't savour the tiny everyday processes that lead to it. I call it **Obsessive Attachment to the Dish and Subconscious Detachment with its Recipe**.

Take for instance, you want to lose weight and look chiselled. You take expert guidance, browse the internet, read books and blogs, ask your peers and finally chalk out a strategy. Let's assume this translates to a work out of 45 minutes a day. Most of us after the first or second day, start posing in front of mirror to look for visible changes knowing fully that it takes time. That's because we are so attached to the mental picture of how we want to look Vs. how we are manifesting everyday. Fast forward 10 days, the results may still not be encouraging and you gradually begin to hate the process. That's how your mind can enslave you of its thoughts.

Instead, *how about treating everyday processes as tiny goals and be jubilant of nailing them each day regarding it as a win!* This win gives us the confidence to march ahead with zeal. Once you dispassionately detach yourself from goals and ferociously attach with the process, the 'Final Goal' will come hunting you down.

Hunt you down it surely will. But these final goals are not so final. The success is not so an end state and the pinnacle you reach is not so the highest you can get yet. Life is a roller-coaster ride giving you unimaginable jolts when you least expect and unfathomable joy when you least desire. Should you, then, be a happiness seeker all the time? We will answer that next.

7 THE GREAT SYNDROME OF ENDLESS UTOPIA

> **"Happiness is a gift and the trick is not to expect it but to delight in it when it comes".**
>
> **– Charles Dickens**

Much clichéd as it may seem, the phrase "**Change is the Only Constant**" has so much to teach us and literally touches every walk of our lives; Be it health, finances, happiness or sorrows, success or setbacks and what have you!

A genuine soul searching would reveal that most of us throughout the day are either brooding over our pasts or are anxious/excited of our future, never caring a damn about what lies in the present, right here, right now! Our bodies are physically present but minds loitering all over the universe. For instance, while brushing out teeth, we are already thinking of what we want to eat for breakfast, while grabbing a bite, our minds are already down the road to our work places, while driving down, we are already planning for who to meet, what to do, how to impress our boss or a colleague and on reaching work place, our minds are already planning for what's the plan for lunch break and this goes on and on and on! Your body is catching up with your mind which is on a sprint 24x7. The worst part of such habits manifests in our conversations. We are never ears to what the other person is saying because our mind is in its own trip and sure enough we become atrocious listeners which, contrary to what we believe, never goes unnoticed.

The point I am trying to make is simply this – we are never ever mentally present in the 'NOW' to savour what life offers. It is worth pondering why most of us have this tendency. And the rationale I am going to suggest now will for sure expose many of our wounds (which most of us will deny) but I do hope with all humility that it heals them too in the process. We as humans want to remain in an ***endless loop of utopia*** which is characterised by good health forever, success after success and happiness being piled up every day till we breathe our last. Sadly, by the very design of nature, this is impossible which is why we are either retrospecting about the past or planning for future all the time so that our loop (an imaginary and impossible loop) is fixed. Yet it never will, never will! The truth is that we will continue to have Highs and Lows throughout our lives and the only low which must concern all of us is our death. In this age of dramatic distraction which has metamorphosed us into ***Digital parasites enslaved to our devices,*** never has it been so urgent to come to terms with the fact that enjoying and savouring the present is more important than anything at all. Like another clichéd phrase, *'Life or success is a journey and not a destination'* it's high time we realise its worth.

It takes courage to accept that success or happiness is not permanent and heart to realise that sorrows are short-lived. We must have the maturity to enjoy the present, be proud of our pasts and be less anxious of our future. Only then will we enjoy brushing our teeth to feel fresh, savour every bite of our breakfast, enjoy the journey enroute to office and put in our heart and soul at work! The endless utopia is an illusion. It never existed and it never will.

8 REVAMP YOUR 'TO-DO LIST'

I just happened to stumble upon the aforementioned quote by Rummer Willis which tossed me into a philosophical trance of sorts only to be shaken up by a phone call. As clichéd as it may seem, yet, there are only a handful of humans who literally walk this talk and how! I must again confess that even I am a work-in-progress about this notion. But it doesn't absolve us from fathoming the gravity of it, does it?

An average human being today (unless he has woken up to this reality in life) says what he feels and does what he says (NOT always though) based entirely on another person's or a group's opinion to which he/she belongs. Perhaps the strongest of all desires for most humans is the 'Need to Belong'. During pre-historic times, it was a necessity; Today, it's a pure selfish-desire. Why else would terms like FOMO (Fear of Missing Out) be coined? For all those who desperately want to break out of this shackle and lead a life you always dreamt of, Good News! It ain't difficult at all.

Consider this simple theory – Whatever you do will fall under these 3 categories:-

#1 What you Ought to Do – This is the highest level a human can reach. NOT at all easy but NOT always difficult. It will hurt many irrational souls but soothe yours. If all have the courage to embrace this, and are surrounded by people who do this, it's the best environment to be in any organisational set-up or even for that matter, a family.

#2 What you Want to Do – This has an element of selfish-motive to it. Relatively easy because *YOU* are your *TOP PRIORITY* and nothing else (read no one else) matters. Many a times, it can coincide with the first category which is super-ideal. But if you are from the former category stuck around a bunch of latter, it's the worst environment to be. Go check out any famous company or a sporting team or dissect any family feud,it most often results from the inability of the team members to identify a common cause and the obsession to serve their personal agenda.

#3 What you are Expected to Do – This is by far the most self-sabotaging category. Your entire being or behaviour feeds on other people's opinions. You are anxious about what you feel, say or do out of fear of being judged and hence tread cautiously till you are old enough to say *IDGAF*!

Let's demystify it with an instance ……

You must remain hail and healthy (What you Ought To Do) but have an obsession with junk and unhealthy food (what you Want To Do) and hence decide to procrastinate working out while continuing to consume all the riff-raff that comes your way because that's what you must do to stay/belong to a group which you love to hang around with (What you are Expected To Do). Long story short, an ideal mix would be to perfectly coincide the first two categories – the *OUGHTS* and *WANTS* and at the same time '*EXPECT*' others to follow it while NOT judging if they don't.

It's high time we re-define our *To-Do List*. An ideal and self-sustaining To-Do List. And once you revamp and redefine it, a strange joy dawns upon you. A joy almost inconceivable; A joy best felt than spoken. Let's discover how in the next chapter.

9

THE ECSTACY OF OPINION-FREE LIFE

It might come as a shock to realise that most humans today act simply on the terms curated by their surroundings. *Before every action done or words uttered, you mentally run through the motions of probable response it would attract from the so-called environment.* We become **validity-seekers** every waking hour and sure enough, also become a slave of their thoughts. Every opinion of others, be it from relatives or friends or colleagues or bosses seem to consume your thought process literally the whole day like a termite gradually eating away a wooden block. Thus, *you subconsciously become a **robot of their choice**.* In military terms, *you become a product whose 'Service Qualitative Requirements' are written by your environment and NOT you.* Though undesirable, yet most of us continue to play in this zone today. It's worth deconstructing this **Opinion-based Behavioural Syndrome** ailing us.

To say that I am not influenced at all by the opinions of environment would be lying-through-my teeth.

While I am no expert, the following analogy would be a great tool to unshackle yourselves and lead a joyful life. There are two kinds of people in our lives – **Well-Wishers** and **Naysayers**. Well-wishers always want the best for you; they rejoice your success, correct your choices out of sheer concern and support your actions. Naysayers always want the best for themselves, seldom rejoice your success, correct your choices so that it feeds their ego and always have an alternative action to every action of yours. Close your eyes for a few seconds and you will visualise pictures of certain individuals flashing back and forth in each category. The simple mantra, in my humble view is to *Embrace the Well-Wisher* and *Ignore the Naysayer*. As long as your words and actions are based on '**What is right**' and '**What is Humane**' and are driven by kindness and selflessness, the Naysayers shouldn't bother you at all. You can safely turn a blind eye and deaf ears to them and still rock this world and your work places.

It's our moral obligation to base all our actions mostly on our own belief system and to an extent on our well-wishers' opinions in order to walk into this world and truly express our potential. *The tricky part however, I must admit, is identifying and categorising individuals into the aforesaid two categories.*

With the current Global Outreach fuelled by internet and social media, every *Inspired Human Being* can Inspire a Million more. Given the global population today, it needs no more than about 8000 souls to uplift the entire world. Yet, it's a far cry from reality because an equal number of souls are engaged in de-inspiring all those around them – either by their deeds, words or responses. Yet, I am hopeful that if we succeed in rightly categorising such individuals, you will be amazed to see how stress-free, decluttered and joyful your life turns out to be. Let me suggest a simple exercise. Make a list of all people who you have regular interaction with and classify them as under:-

Well-Wishers	Naysayers	Your Actions
		• Be brutally honest in listing out. Even if it means someone very close to you.
		• Base 80% of your interactions with Well-wishers.
		• Do not share your visions and ideas with naysayers as they will de-inspire you.

Once you base your behaviour and interaction on the aforesaid dictum, it's almost surprising how your productivity and impact grows exponentially at your work places, friend circles and family.

We will now see who is the one person in this world who you must always satisfy, no matter what.

10 WORK FOR YOUR OWN UNIQUE SATISFACTION

> **"Working for Success will make you a Master;**
> **But working for satisfaction will make you a legend".**
>
> **– Anonymous**

Each one of us has a **unique set of enduring beliefs that define us** as an individual. Although, some are inherited directly from our parents, they are *continuously harnessed, revised and refined till our last breath* but remain unique in every way because our life experiences and environments are unique. Having said that, isn't **it an irony that most of us still try and apply the template of happiness, satisfaction and joy of others onto us?** It's never worked. It never will! *A professionally successful person might have a horrendous domestic front and likewise an average soul might be a Man-Friday for his/her family. The reverse may well be the case too!* I am not even saying which is right or wrong and even the so called *'Strike-a-Balance'* is a cliché because **our professional and personal aspirations bloat out of proportions as we grow older, often in opposite directions**. Many of us spend our entire lives solving this Jigsaw Puzzle only to realise that it's about 30 years too late! *The solution lies in redefining the whole raison d'etre of being which with all humility may I confess, is easier said than done.* The key to remain happy, satisfied and motivated is to **work for your own satisfaction which is again a product of your belief system, a *Unique Belief***

System Indeed! The only catastrophe we all quite easily fall prey is to get too attached with results and outcomes. We are way too much of an incentive driven creatures often subconsciously chanting *'What's in it for Me?'* for every act. As alluded to in the earlier chapter on detachment, much to the disbelief of many, *'Process'* was, is and will always remain more crucial than immediate outcomes. Another eye-opener to ponder is that most of our work-related stress is due to 'fear of being judged' by all and sundry as a means to threaten our aspirations. **It's worth realising that many a times you won't get the due or credit you deserve in terms of promotion or pay rise or position or grades but the applause you receive from all those around you as a result of your deeds is always priceless and no award can match it**. Intangibles always outweigh the tangibles. Yet, it's the tangibles that drive most of our behaviours today. This must change and change for good.

As responsible humans, if we can inspire everyone around us, leave everyone who meets us happier than before and exude positive vibes by our very presence, we don't need medals to prove our worth! You see, ***it's better to deserve a medal and not have it than have it and not deserve it. Work for your own unique satisfaction!***

11 TRUE METRIC OF SUCCESS

WHAT THE SOCIETY SELLS YOU

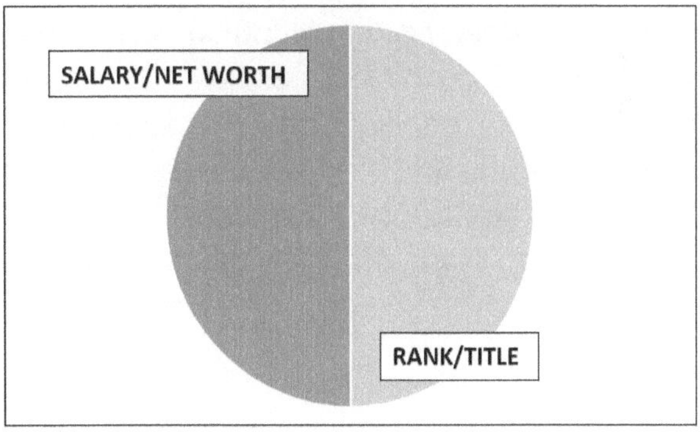

THE TRUTH WE REFUSE TO ACCEPT

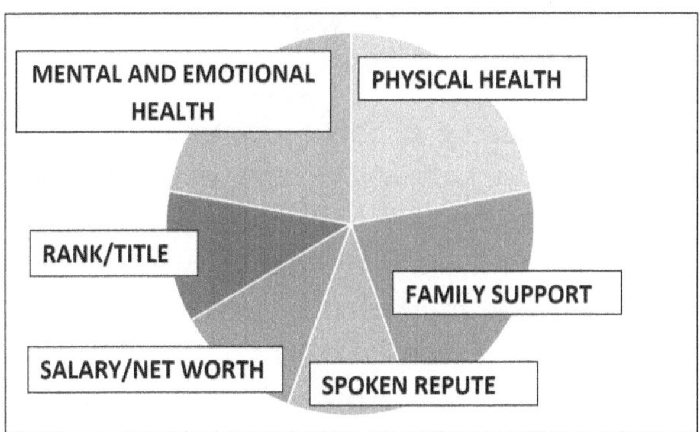

Having understood what success is constituted of, it's also important to know, then, what competence is all about and how most of us have got it all wrong.

12 MISPLACED CONCEPT OF PROFESSIONAL COMPETENCE

We often attribute the phrase *"Professional Competence"* to someone who has done well in competitive or qualification exams and such other academic pursuits. If this is to be believed in letter and spirit, please explain to me why some of these so called Professionally Competent souls fail miserably in delivering on ground and why few others who are branded *Incompetent* by the same (misplaced) yardstick create wonders and end up being **Man-Fridays for their leaders at every level**. It's high time we do a genuine soul searching to fathom its true connotation.

Let us demystify it ......

What we commonly call Professional Competence is in essence "**Academic Excellence**". Very few of us realise that the latter is a subset of the former much in contrary to the popular belief of them being synonymous.

Academic Excellence is about cramming up answers to the point and scoring marks. Professional Competence is about delivering the desired results when it matters by taking mature decisions and standing up for what is right. Sure enough, some degree of academic excellence is *sine qua non* for competence but it won't always guarantee the same. **It's our moral obligation to turn our academic pursuits into professional competence and not rest on laurels which are purely academic in flavour.**Given a choice, which category would you prefer in your team? A good student or a good teacher (read *leader*)? **A Professionally Competent**

or an Academically Excellent Subordinate? Given the environmental realities today, **our obvious choice is easiest to pick, yet hardest to admit!**

Let's dig deeper. Professional competence, in my humble view, is an amalgam of the three closely inter-related and symbiotic facets that carve your personality. They are – **Academic Excellence**, **Leadership Skills** and **Professional Conduct** at your work places or organisation, so to speak. The real growth as a leader lies at the intersect of these three facets. This zone of coincidence, I would like to call it as a **Growth Bubble**. Larger the bubble, greater the growth. In other words, greater is your impact on your team and on your subordinates. You will often see many individuals being exceptional in one of them while being pitiful in others. You can ill afford to be unidimensional, can you? To be impactful is to embrace all three of them and forever strive to enlarge the Growth Bubble. And like you, me and most of humans today, we are all *work-in-progress* and this world thrives on those who seek growth and progress. Not on those who keep shrinking their Growth Bubbles! Have a look at the model below:-

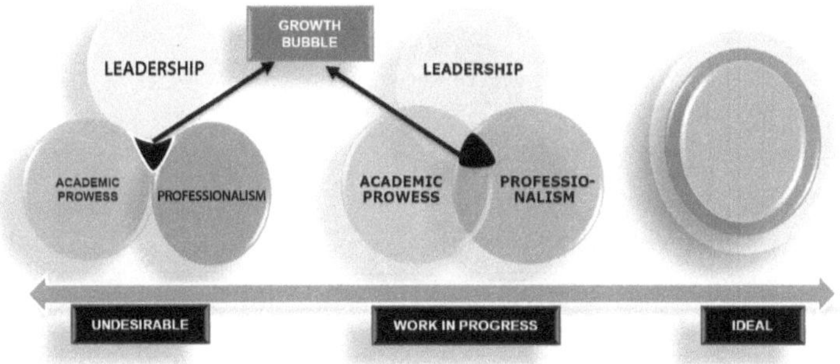

But then, like all disruptive ideas border on counter intuition, there is something I wish to share and exhort all those who want to be impactful and usher in '*real change*' and a *cultural renaissance* at your work places. It's a method which most would dismiss as an act of cowardice. Most would also dismiss it labelling it as being submissive and servile. Yet, a large part of me is confident that it has all it takes to grow you and your team exponentially. Let's take you to the next chapter for that.

13 WAIT FOR YOUR TURN!

> **"God, grant me the SERENITY to accept the things I can't change; COURAGE to change the things I can; and WISDOM to know the difference".**
>
> **– Serenity Prayer**

Of all the marvellous and unimaginable possibilities, our planet earth and humankind has to offer, if there's one thing that may never reach its ultimate destination, it is this – **Idealism** and **Perfectionism**. *There is no human who's perfect and no teams or organisations that are ideal*, so to speak. NOT because cruelty has reached its zenith; NOT because no organisation has a conducive environment anymore; BUT because, like I keep saying, we are all '**Work in Progress**' and the very desire to be ideal and perfect is itself a process of joy and satisfaction. If we all genuinely come to terms with this fact, it must really surprise you as to how many souls get disillusioned on joining a new team or organisation or a job when their expectations and desires take a beating.

Let's take this simple instance. *Say, you join a new company of 50 odd employees. On joining, you are taken aback to learn that most people around are engulfed in financial irregularities, ethical blunders driven by a slender moral fibre. Three options are open to you.* **Option A** *– Accept it as a norm and join the party.* **Option B** *– Refuse to accept and revolt whilst standing for a cause.* **Option C** *– Accept it as fate, don't indulge yourself in such* *pursuits, but don't revolt as you can influence a lot once you are at the helm. Apprising you the benefits of Option C is the burden of this chapter.* Let's deconstruct all the three.

Option A is the easiest of all as being partner in crime has its own perks because you belong to the violent majority. However, Option B doesn't guarantee success! In the instant case, say, *if you are against rest of the 49 or in best case scenario, it's 10 vs 40, you are more likely to be ousted from the team as silent majority and left to fend for yourself and worse still, you could hardly bring about any change to your team's larger good.* How inspiring is it for all those around you? and above all, how big a difference did you make to your organisation? I dare say, *Zilch!* It's the Option C that's real jackpot! Something which very few are courageous enough to accept. ***Option B is, with all due respect, a twisted honour! An honour which is inconsequential and uninspiring in many ways***.

As you go through the hierarchy of your organisation rising high through whatever (ethical) metric, your circle of influence goes from ZERO on your first day to MYRIAD based on where you reach. *If you make a note of all that's bothering you and choose NOT to revolt BUT to change when you're the boss at whatever level, imagine how many lives you will eventually end up touching and inspiring and how gigantic will be the difference you would have made to your organisation or team!* **Compare Options B and C and their respective aftermaths and your heart will pop-out yelling the truth.**

If at all you want to make a difference, **wait for your turn!**

I must admit, however, that its easier said than done. Not all of us can tread through such an inhospitable and unsatisfactory environment full of jolts of disillusionment. Not all of us can sit back and let it pass in the hope that you will remain unscathed. Not all of us have the patience to wait for bigger changes to manifest. And above all, not all have the humility to supress their egos and accept what they can change and what they can't. It's for such souls and many other impactful humans that I offer a short prayer that follows at the end of part II. A prayer which pours out my feelings in the hope that such humans and leaders won't quit influencing and inspiring their spheres of influence.

14 THE REAL WORK-LIFE BALANCE

> "I get asked about work-life balance all the time. And in my view, that's a debilitating phrase because it implies there's a strict trade-off. I rather envision a more holistic relationship between the two. If I am happy at home, I come to office with tremendous energy and If I am happy at work, I come home with tremendous energy. This work-life harmony is what I try to teach young employees and actually senior executives at Amazon too".
>
> – Jeff Bezos

We often hear people advising us to strike a balance between professional and personal life for a happy living. Yet, you will rarely find people who implement it in its truest sense. I think of it as a fallacy of sorts because they aren't independent of each other in water tight compartments and I dare say, they profoundly influence each other in many many ways.

The balance is necessary but not between the aforesaid two but with the quality of work you produce. An illustration of the same will make it amply clear.

Supposing, you are given a task by your superior to prepare a feedback or a presentation during the daytime office hours and are asked to show the same the next day. However, you also promised your wife and kids to take them out for a dinner or you have invited some of your friends at your place for dinner or simpler still, you promised your little kid for swimming classes at the pool in the evening.

You have two choices – Either to slog it out overnight and produce a masterpiece which automatically means you will have to cancel all your commitments or to produce something of a reasonably presentable standard which means you still have time for all your personal commitments.

The former choice will definitely make your superior extremely happy and will earn you accolades albeit with minor amends which he is bound to make. But deep down in your heart, you would wish you hadn't cancelled your personal commitments. This stems directly from the fact that most of us who are in hierarchical set up of an organisation are too cautious and apprehensive of what our bosses will think of our work and hence constantly engage ourself in a never-ending game of perfection, little realising that **Perfectionism only makes us feel Inadequate and Not Perfect**.

However, the latter choice may not entirely make your superior very happy but he will still give a pat on your back, make a couple of additional changes and you are game. And deep down, your level of professional and personal satisfaction will know no bounds. And what's more ! you would still have that room for improvement by waking up a little early the next day and working on it before finally presenting it.

Well, I must admit, it isn't as easy as it seems because often you get worried of the quality of work but through consistent practice you will definitely attain mastery over it and enjoy a healthy family life too. Thus, this is the real balance which is simple yet uncommonly understood by most of us. Only then, as Jeff Bezos says, can you reach home from office smiling and happy and reach office from home energised and full of enthusiasm. Well, may I remind you, it's not only upto the employees to strike this harmony or balance but also equally upto those leaders in authority to ensure they don't expect perfection or go bonkers when any work produced by their subordinates doesn't fit into their definition of *'Good Work'*. An issue closely related to work-life balance is our desire to be exceptional which never comes without a cost; a cost whose worthiness often seems elusive. Is it a good deal to be exceptional? Let's answer that in next chapter.

15 THE PRICE OF EXCEPTIONALISM

It only takes a little common sense (albeit uncommon today) to realise that overdoing anything has its own side-effects. Now, that could be medication or habits or even being workaholic or perfectionist. *It's absolutely OK to be striving for excellence in our careers but most of us don't define the costs and as a result, the first things that get thrown out the window are our personal pursuits* (including family life).

If you want to be exceptional in your career, you have got to goddamn give it all, don't you? You got to slog 80 hours a week to be heads and shoulders above your competitors. Say, you want to be a scientist or a simply a front runner in everything you do – You need to crank out every single day because that's the price you got to pay. *The harsh truth about this is that it makes you very unidimensional. And mind you, this is the only way to be if your aim is to be at the zenith till your last breath.* However, in this pursuit, you may get success but you won't get a life. It takes a whole chunk of your personal life including family and friends to achieve that. *The sacrifices are disproportionate to satisfaction.*

On the other hand, consider having a wholesome life wherein you take off enough time in the day or week to pursue your hobbies or hang out with friends and family which, if done regularly, may obviate a desperate need for vacation altogether! Exceptionalism or Perfectionism aims at achieving 200% in one dimension (all others being fate accompli) whereas a wholesome life aims at 80 % in 4-5 dimensions. Which of the two you think is more satisfying and richer in terms of experiencing the gift of life? Once you are old enough to say 'Been there, done that', which of two memories would you cherish more? *You now have your answer.*

16 SELF CONFIDENCE: AN EXTERNAL PROCESS

We all talk so glibly about this aspect of *'Self Confidence'* these days. Everyone around us, be it teachers or mentors or self-styled motivational speakers, *urge us to develop self-confidence but few tell us HOW?* Many of us also firmly believe that self-confidence is an entirely internal process and we are the whole sole bastions of nurturing it. It's far from being true!

Self-Confidence is largely founded on the response of the external environment; the way you are treated by your peers and superiors, the way they define you as an individual in a particular group or an organisation and above all, the quality of encouragement and inspiration you draw from your external ecosystem. Consider this analogy – *A child doesn't know a thing about self-confidence, yet through constant encouragement by parents and teachers (of course backed by tons of pampering!), the child begins to develop and nurture self-confidence, layer-by-layer, brick-by-brick. The actual acquisition and harnessing of skill-set and competence only happens much later based on this foundation defined largely by the child's external environs.* It's anybody's guess as to what would be the fate of a child who is constantly reminded of his/her shortcomings. The child will subconsciously define itself as a recipe of failure, let alone building self-confidence! Similar analogy applies to all of us as well. *Why else do most of us get discouraged or disheartened when our ideas or perceptions are shot down (more so when done publicly) by our peers or superiors?* It does dent our self-confidence, doesn't it?

Whether we like it or not, even *we are responsible for shaping self-confidence of all those around us. Every statement or comment made by us, sincere or insincere, genuine or sarcastic, either augments or harms another person's self-confidence.* In any organisation, it's our moral obligation to keep encouraging and inspiring everyone around us and develop an environment conducive to growth through self-confidence. They say, people don't leave bad companies, they leave bad leaders. How very true. So, you see, it ain't entirely an internal process!

A very strange but rather a welcome side-effect of self-confidence is an enhanced competitiveness through competence – largely a product of how you have been groomed as a leader and a subordinate by your own leaders. The catch however here is that the competition it ushers in is healthy as it defies all other classical definitions of competition. We will see how.

17 THE ONLY HEALTHY COMPETITION!

> **"I am in competition with no one. I run my own race. I have no desire to play the game of being better than anyone in any way, shape or form. I just aim to improve, to be better than I was before. That's me and I am free".**
>
> **– Jenny Perry**

We keep hearing this clichéd phrase of *'Competition with Self'* as the key to success as opposed to *'Competing with Others'*. Well, it won't hurt to deconstruct its truth.

When you compete with others, you *subconsciously always aim to defeat your opponent rather than winning.* This ambitious aim translates into many a damaging attitude like *jealousy, hatred, inferiority* (or *superiority*) *complex, inflated ego* or *self-doubt.* The worst part is that *all of this happens subconsciously without your consent and even realisation! You may win but will never be satisfied which is worse than losing.*

On the other hand, when you compete with yourself (former/younger self or previous standards), *you subconsciously always aim at winning rather than defeating.* This inspirational aim translates into many a constructive attitude like *self-love, self-confidence, large heartedness, being accommodative to others, humility* and being *ever pumped up with energy and inspiration* (more so because your own self must be bettered now). The best part is that *all of this happens subconsciously without your consent and even realisation! You may not always win but will always be satisfied which is a zillion time better than winning and quite often leads to consistency in success.*

Anything based on the foundations of knocking down your opponent does not yield long lasting inspiration. Take for instance *the Great Titanic.* This ship was built amidst intense rivalry and competition amongst various ship builders. So much was her self-inflated supremacy that the owner said '*Even God Can't Sink this Ship*' and we all know what happened on her very first voyage!

The only competition that's healthy is with yourself!

18 THE ONLY PLACE TO PUNCH BELOW OUR WEIGHTS

None can disagree with the fact that every ounce of growth or improvement we all have experienced ever since our births (and so shall it be till we breathe our last) has been a result of expanding or pushing our limits in whichever area we wanted to excel. We got our dues only when we punched above our weights! *Expanding your limits is all about building that everlasting trust with yourself which doesn't develop overnight but is built layer by layer for every such act of pushing your limits until it's strong enough to overwhelm you with its impact.* We talk about building trust with our colleagues, superiors and subordinates. In any organisation, you take months and years to develop that trust in others through relentless hardwork, sense of belongingness and dedication which, once developed, will spread faster than virus (*read spoken reputation*) before you reach a new place.

That being said, aren't we equally accountable to build that trust with our inner selves? Every small act of pushing your limits adds that layer of trust with yourself which when accumulated over a period of time can transform you to unimaginable proportions and make you reach unsurmountable heights. All because you took an inch extra every single time! Isn't this amazing?

So, next time you are on a 5km run, run a couple of 100 yards extra with same intensity and collapse (I bet you won't!)

When you plan on reading till 11 pm, read for about 15mins more!

When you plan to do 20 push ups or sit ups, push your way through for another 5!

When you plan to wake up by 5 am, go an inch extra by keeping your alarm at 4:45 am and don't snooze!

When you are tempted to have candies or sweets or overeat because it's your favourite dish but you know you need to keep your weight in check, eat a candy less or sometimes go an inch extra by not having at all!

When a boxer gets knocked down in the ring, it's his will and not skill that will enable him get up every single time! All because he went an inch extra everyday in his practice sessions!

All these small acts of pushing your limits are actually *little acts of kindness* you do for yourself to develop that battle-proofed trust (much like inter-personal relations as above) and willpower which will make you fundamentally a different and a transformed human being; a person who doesn't blink an eye when confronted with a crisis. And what's more! such attitudes are contagious especially if you are a *Team Leader* at any level.

The only place we all can afford to punch below our weights without incurring losses is the weighing machine!

So far we have seen many a counterintuitive approaches to building self-confidence, being competitive, building that trust with yourself by relentlessly sticking to the process while detaching from the end states, enhancing professional competence, defining our to-do lists and above all, working for our own unique satisfaction while being dispassionately unshackled from the opinion of others. But for all of these to even begin manifesting in our lives, we need a strong foundation; A foundation without which it's impossible for you to be inspirational and impactful at any place you are planted. Rather, it's the very ingredient that lets you bloom where you are planted. We will see what and why it is *everything* in the next chapter.

19 REASON IS EVERYTHING

A human being for whatever his/her worth irrespective of profession should first of all establish and also believe WHY he does what he does. *If the WHY is clear, the HOW becomes a cake-walk!* The thematic premise of this 'why' is driven by two kinds of Motivation – **Extrinsic** and **Intrinsic**. An individual with Extrinsic motivation does what he does in order to fit into the realms of external environs whereas an intrinsically motivated individual does so in order to uphold his own personal values and lofty standards he has set for himself.

Consider these hypothetical examples of **John** and **Kim** –

John would never misbehave with a girl or indulge in any sort of forceful ventures because he respects the dignity of a Woman just as any other human being whereas Kim wouldn't dare do to so because he fears punishment or imprisonment.

John would always strive hard to contribute positively at his work place because he has a deep sense of belongingness to his organisation and shares his vision with his boss whereas Kim does so because he wants to

reach higher positions and ranks real quick and make lots of money and fame.

 # John shows relentless dedication and sincerity in his work always and everytime because he believes in ownership of the tasks assigned whereas Kim does so with extra energy whenever he is under observation or scrutiny because he never wants to miss a chance to impress his boss.

 # John drops a simple text wishing his boss on his birthday or anniversary or wishes in person if feasible because he knows the difference between genuine wishes and flattery whereas Kim sends flowers and gifts and also makes it a point to wish personally with a cosmetic grandeur because he knows most humans fall for flattery.

 # John stays up late at office when circumstances are inevitable and carry home some of it if to entails some discomfort to others who're stuck around him due to protocols whereas Kim stays up late even when circumstances aren't inevitable, calls up his boss thrice making foolish queries just to let him know he is still at office and make the whole subordinate staff wait in the bargain.

In all these cases, Kim is doing the right things for the wrong reasons while John is doing the right things for the obvious reasons. John's motivation is intrinsic and hence long-lasting whereas that of Kim's is extrinsic and hence temporary and transactional. At any work place or an organisation, both the kinds of people are easily discernible even by a person of lowest IQ (say, a watchman). WHY you do what you do is more important than what you do. **Define your reason and be committed to it.**

To continue to do your best in perfect alignment with your raison d'etre, to continue to shine and bloom where you are planted and be a game changer in this world and above all, to continue to be a splendid human being who exudes positive energy every waking hour, you need but one ingredient to be 'Glass Full' than any other. Let's discover that in next chapter.

20 INSPIRATION ISN'T PERMANENT

> "People often say that motivation doesn't last. Well, neither does bathing – that's why we recommend it daily".
>
> – Zig Ziglar

We all talk quite glibly about this term called '*Inspiration*' and opine that we must stay inspired at work and also inspire all those around us. However, the way it manifests is a far cry from our popular beliefs. Most of us know '*What it is*' but few have contemplated on '*How to Nurture it*'.

I know for a fact that we don't wake up each day *Super-Excited* and turn up *Ultra-Inspired* to our work places. I am sure you will appreciate it too. Our minds are way too complicated to ensure this permanency automatically. Take for instance, your own profession – *Are you excited and inspired to the same magnitude and intensity as that of day one of your job*? You have your answer. Well, let's not be too harsh on ourselves and feel blameworthy for it as science defines this phenomenon as '***Hedonic Adaptation***'. It's a phenomenon due to which our minds return to a stable level of happiness set-point after a while despite major success or setbacks (yes, it's equally true for negativities!). **To a layman, it simply means inspiration is a fuel which drains over time and hence needs regular refuelling.**

The only practical way of keeping that fuel level to optimum is to populate your minds with positive and inspiring thoughts on a daily basis. No matter how busy we are, it's our moral obligation to read about war heroes, business tycoons, magical doctors, exemplary teachers and self-less social workers, watch documentaries of how humans across the globe have defied all odds to carve a niche for all of us to follow suit, listen to podcasts of famous personalities who unshackle you from victimhood and enable you lead a life of extraordinary possibilities.

For instance, watching a few minutes of interview or speeches of giants like Fd Masrhal Maneckshaw or APJ Abdul Kalam or Rata Tata or Mother Teresa or more contemporarily, Jeff Bezos or Elon Musk alone can sky-rocket your spirits for days. Our Body is a vehicle and our mind its engine. **The quality of fuel (and of course the frequency of re-fuelling) you feed dictates your productivity and hence the quality of life**. The quote by Zig Ziglar above says it all! *How often do you Re-fuel?*

That brings us to the end of Part-I which, as I said earlier, is an essential pre-requisite to be able to dive deep, discover and deconstruct the next part. Hope it resonated with your deepest beliefs.

PART II

DECONSTRUCT TRUE LEADERSHIP

Disclaimer Alert!

I would be lying through my teeth and fooling everyone around me and more importantly, myself if I claim to be even an inch closer to being a Leadership Guru. I am NOT. Nor do I intend to. In fact, few can profess and declare to have seen it all and been it all because each one of us have such diverse and unique experiences in our personal and professional journeys that 'One Size Fits All' approach is rarely profitable. Yet, I firmly believe there are few bare essentials of a leader in any field that are sine qua non for a team to even be happy and motivated, let alone succeed. What I am going to share in the upcoming chapters is borne out of only two aspects – 'What I expect from my leader' and 'What I am as a leader'. Many may not find it comfortable to flip through the following chapters of this part if my concepts and stances don't fit into their definition of a leader. Yet, if you have the courage and humility to embrace it all, you will be transformed. So, be advised.

21 AFFIRMATION PRAYER OF A TRUE LEADER

Affirmations have always been found to be phenomenally helpful in shaping behaviours of us humans who are gifted with an intelligent brain as opposed to primitive brains of all other creatures. Be it *Dr Norman Vincent Peale* or *Dr Joseph Murphy* or many other psychologists today, all of them have professed this to be a powerful tool to achieve literally anything ethical you desire because it targets your subconscious minds. So, before we even begin deconstructing what true leadership is all about, let me walk you through a powerful affirmation which I read everyday before I walk out of my house to enable me inch closer to True and Impactful Leadership.

I am an Impactful Leader.

I am Kind and Compassionate.

I do not exploit obedience of my subordinates to fillip my growth.

I do not have unreasonable demands which are not in the larger interest of my organisation.

I ensure that the job is done as it ought to be done and NOT as I want it to be done.

I am a Good Listener.

I don't use my team as a stepping stone.

My whims and fancies have lowest priority in my work ethics.

\# I am Duty-Conscious and NOT Privilege-Conscious.

\# I am not a parasite to my team.

\# My team gets inspired by my very presence.

\# My attitude and empathy is world-class.

\# I am a wonderful human being.

First things first and best things first, we will now dig deep on a trait which, if a leader doesn't embody, it doesn't matter what else he embodies, it's rarely impactful.

22 DECODING SELFLESSNESS

Dr APJ Abdul Kalam aka Missile Man of India is by far one of the most revered leaders world over in modern times. Every word uttered by him rallied along millions of followers and his every action is still being taken as a *Datum of Deeds*. Such a rare amalgam he was – A Scientist, a Statesman and a humble Human. Yet, it's amazing how with great humility he admitted that much of his selflessness was learnt from seniors in his field. In 2008, I had the opportunity to attend a lecture by the Missile Man to all NDA Cadets on the occasion of our *Diamond Jubilee*. He shared an interesting anecdote which goes as follows.

Back in July 1979, when SLV-3 (Satellite Launch Vehicle) was being planned for a launch, everyone in the team at SHAR (Satish Dhawan Space Centre, Shriharikota) were super-excited and anxious at the same time. So was the entire nation for here we were, barely over a quarter of a century post independence,aspiring to make a mark in the extra-terrestrial space. Come the D Day for the launch, all checks and balances were in place. *Three, two, one* and here it soared into heavens, or so we thought. It instead made its way to Bay of Bengal! Post this debacle which had incurred an expenditure of approximately Rs 20 Crores, Kalam, being the Project Director was prepping up for the Press Conference to confront a Barrage of Hows and Whys from the elite news reporters. Just then, Satish Dhawan suddenly appeared back stage and informed that he would face the press and did it so very passionately taking all the blame onto himself.

Come the next launch date, July 1980, all the faults had been rectified with calculations having more than doubled to ensure clock work precision. Three, two, one and once again the LV soared high, this time flirting (yet not embracing) with Bay of Bengal and successfully reaching outer space. Needless to say, the team was flooded with congratulatory messages pouring in from lengths and breadths of the nation. Understandably, from previous experience though, Kalam sat back relaxed assuming Satish Dhawan to be taking on the Press Conference. But that wasn't to be. He instead asked Kalam to head the Press Conference and gave full credit to him. Nothing explains Selflessness better than this anecdote. No wonder, such attitudes are contagious.

Selflessness is a hallmark of a good and impactful human being. Many of us engage it symbolically, few others don't even bother trying while many have made it a way of their lives. When it comes to understanding the essence of this term 'Selflessness' most of us get it completely wrong. *Most popular notion of this term is that you sacrifice everything in your life for your family and well-wishers and lead a life of Monk-of-Sorts.* The reality is a far cry from this notion.

In my humble view, selflessness is a concern for the larger good than the personal gains. It signifies how much you value **'WE'** than **'ME'** when it comes to your actions or words at your work places or family fronts. Be it an organisation or a family, you will find both these types of individuals. The funny part, however, is that both the clans are successful. In fact, the latter is able to succeed with more consistency. It's worth dissecting the minds of both these clans as that's where the answer to our question (who exactly is a Selfless Man?) lies.

'ME' types have a personal agenda to be followed in letter and spirit and always urge their subordinates indirectly (some even directly) to align themselves with them. *They have a personal bucket list to tick every waking hour which ensures their success.* **Any success to their team is purely co-incidental and NOT intended**. *They are fiercely addicted to quick-fixes which puts a price tag on their values, honesty and integrity. Worse still, they even attempt to brainwash all and sundry with the notion that all these values are a mere 'Lack of Opportunity'. They may personally win every single race they run BUT are all alone on the track with none to cheer. They eventually end up disillusioned irrespective of where they reach. Their subordinates obey them because they* **'have to'** *and breathe a sigh of relief on their departure.*

On the other hand, **'WE'** type individuals are a lot different. **Their minds just can't conceive the idea of 'Personal Perks'. Their whole concept and efforts are directed towards uplifting their teams while in the bargain, they uplift their own self-esteem**. They have visions and goals for their team and their bucket list flows out of it. **Any personal success is purely co-incidental as they are fiercely addicted to the overall well-being of their team of which 'Good Performance' is a natural fall-out**. They may not win every single race they run BUT are never alone on the track and have a myriad admirers cheering them up. Their subordinates obey them because they **'want to'** and drop tears on their departure as they were deeply touched the whole time!

If modern examples seem more palatable, allow me to throw some light on another luminary named Elon Musk. On 12 June 2014, he declared his electric car's patents open for any company desirous of embracing his technology and design. Yes, you read that right. Any sane and successful entrepreneur would say he's gone nuts. Not until Elon Musk gave this beautiful explanation when asked in one of the interviews about why on earth would someone do such a thing. He likened our world or earth so to speak, to a ship in the ocean (read universe). If, say, there's a hole in the deck of your ship and all on board must show up with whatever container they have, to empty the water oozing out back into the ocean and you have the largest and most efficient buckets with you which can speed up the entire process and thereby saving the ship, would you start selling those buckets? or would you say, "Hey, take this. We are in this together". To be honest, such anecdotes of selflessness and folks with larger cause in mind are very, very rare to come across. But you will know why is Musk one of the wealthiest persons today. If you really want to embrace the idea of 'Selflessness', you don't need to venture into Himalayas or be a Monk. All you need is to be a 'WE' type and Satisfaction(primary) and Success(secondary) will come hunting you down. This applies equally to your family life and relations too.

23 THE BIGGEST GUILT OF A LEADER?

> **"Don't be afraid to ask questions. Don't be afraid to ask for help when you need it. I do that every day. Asking for help isn't a sign of weakness, it's a sign of strength. It shows you have the courage to admit when you don't know something and to learn something new".**
>
> **– Barack Obama**

There are plenty of occasions when we feel stuck at something and our minds just doesn't seem to find an answer. One of the simplest ways is to ask for help. *It could be your significant other, your parents or besties. You will be amazed at how many of them were willing to offer their shoulders to rest but assumed that you just didn't need it!* Corollary is true too. If you ever find someone not okay by their looks or behaviour, ask if they need help. Yet, very few people have the courage to do both and the reason is laughable to say the least.

It takes greater courage, perhaps, if it's your subordinates who you are looking up to leaning on. Well, I have come across such a courageous leader. But before I share this inspirational and thought provoking anecdote, let me take you a bit deeper into the human brain. Let's fathom its anatomy. It's fascinating to say the least and how. Human brain consists of two identical hemispheres. Further zooming in, we have the hippocampus (responsible for learning and memory) and anterior to the hippocampus in each hemisphere sits a small, almond shaped, cute-little-member called the *Amygdala*. Well, it isn't as cute – It regulates extremities of emotions in our body which involve fear and aggression. In other words, it's the architect of the '*Fight or Flight*' response based on the threat perceived and fed in the form of dense signals from the reasoning headmaster of our brain called the *Pre-frontal Cortex*. The moment we come across something fearful or something agitating enough, the Amygdala kicks-in to regulate your response, famously referred to as the **Amygdala Hijack.** If you have, which I am sure all of us have, come across folks who lose their cool unreasonably and shout at the top of their voices in a jiffy or are unimaginably frightened at slightest of discomfort or threat, blame it on the cutie-pie. Yet, the fact that most humans manage to control their anger or curb their fear itself testifies that both these emotions are a matter of choice and not involuntary. An Amygdala is too small a pry to impact a human being's brain who has even tamed wholly mammoths.

I had one such senior who, I would consider to be one of the most thoroughbred professionals you could ever find. Like all of us have one odd weakness or a drawback, he had one too. But a costly one at that. He had the shortest temper. Or so he chose to have. His brain would shut off like MCP trip wire and he would shout so loud at a person he was admonishing that the whole office complex would hear it. Military has a way to get you to hold positions of authority that, if not nurtured well, can overwhelm you, often manifesting into an autocratic behaviour. My mother always used to say (and even says to this day) – **"If you don't have control over your anger, it really doesn't matter what else you have, it's hard for people to like you or willingly follow you".** Back to this Gentleman, as this scenario went on for months, one fine day, he happened to call me over for some discussion on an upcoming training event which we were entrusted with conducting. Two minutes into our conversation, a soldier walked in with something he had asked for, in a file, which apparently wasn't the thing he had asked for. Such was the fear (and hatred) amongst all about this man that it could, and sometimes did, make a person so conscious and fearful that he often forgot what was ordered by this gentleman. As the wrong file was brought in, Lo and behold, there began the customary barrage of swearing from his own unique repertoire of choicest abuses that can shatter any human being's confidence. I couldn't help but intervene to bail the poor guy out on the pretext that we should concentrate on the important event coming up first and not get distracted with the riff-raff (yes, that's how he referred to them when they acted irresponsibly). I also sent across a word outside to not let anyone in for next 30 minutes so that we could plan and discuss peacefully and keep the gentleman's cute Amygdala at bay! Well, we did plan and discuss a whole lot than we could have imagined. Except that it wasn't about the training exercise. We discussed something I never dreamt of. Life orchestrates such serendipitous associations. The gentleman sitting in front of me, looked into my eyes and before I could say a word, had a drop of tear trickling down his blood red face. You don't see a senior in the Army doing that in front of a subordinate. We are all taught to live by the dictum of Field Marshal Maneckshaw who said *"It's one thing to be angry and fearful and quite another to show it"*. We never expose our follies or confide about our chinks in the armour to our subordinates who are looking upto us for inspiration every waking hour. We are never wired that way. Never built that way. Never lived that way. Yet, here was a courageous soul who chose to confide in a junior and boy! did that conversation of 30 minutes change our lives forever. As tears trickled down, he looked at me with an intense feeling of frustration, fear and helplessness and said "Vishal, I don't like what I do. I hate the moment I spit out anger but it seems as if someone else has the joystick of my behaviour. It's as if I am at a gun point to behave the way I behave". In unsaid words, all he meant was a three word phrase –"Please Help Me". What do you do when a person of that stature comes up to you to seek guidance on an issue which you least expected. He would later disclose that he liked the way I handled things even when the situation is tense and the pressure is intense. I subconsciously added a phrase to the inventory of Maneckshawism –**"It's one thing to admire your subordinate and quite another to tell him upfront".** This gentleman simply testified that irrespective of statures, we are after all, only humans! It takes courage, raw courage to tell that to your subordinate. Close your eyes and try recollecting any instance where in you have wholeheartedly showered praises on your subordinate. You will know why it's so rare and so special, for both the senior and junior.

Like any sane human would respond when asked for help, I did no different. I went about giving my rationale of such behaviour and how one can curb it. Though I explained in detail why we do what we do, the central theme remained same – *Anger is a matter of Choice*. Period. It was a sense of insecurity by and large, that I thought, contributed to our outburst of anger. We are insecure of our own stature and have a constant self-doubt that lurks within that prompts us to believe that people will take you for granted or disobey you. It's insecurity about your own abilities that nurtures a fear within that prompts us to believe that your superiors are judging you and you ain't scoring that well in their report cards. Hence, you pass on that anger onto those around you to relieve yourself. Who you shower bile on also has a lot to say about the whole idea of anger management. It's a fallacy to believe that it ain't under our control. If it really isn't under our control, then please explain to me why don't we burst out on our bosses or seniors or for that matter anyone who is more powerful than us? I am sure, those powerful people piss you off as often as others. Yet, we never loose cool on those who write our appraisals. You hurt only those who are least equipped to hurt you back. That's human tendency. For that matter, the basic tendency of any living creature on earth. But, only humans have the ability to understand that it's a matter of choice. It's the very reason why I am able to think through and pen it down in this book. To realise this itself, is the biggest act of selflessness. To shed the ego, unshackle the insecurity and let go off fake-fear that has befriended our Amygdala. Humans are pretty much equipped to arrest the Amygdala Hijack and it's only a matter of choice and not helplessness. The fact that he occasionally busted out at his wife and children also reinforced my theme. We talked about a whole lot of other things like how to take a pause when angry, which I had learnt over a period of time, the choice of words and how to be empathetic towards our co-workers or subordinates. I couldn't agree more on the common saying that *a conversation can change your life.* These 30 minutes did more than it could for 30 years for that gentleman, as he confessed. And there, he also taught me a rather valuable lesson – *"Don't feel guilty of seeking help, even if it's from a younger human with lesser experience. You never know the power of such conversations".* Today, the officer is a splendid human being enjoying every walk of his life, professional and personal alike. It's as if there were two characters in his life separated by a span of that 30-minute conversation, he says, often, laughingly. I must confess, I was myself bewildered at the impact it had but I guess that's how God helps those who are willing to seek help. I haven't, for once, hesitated to seek help or praise my subordinates, when due, ever since. It's a courageous act.

Well, I have also come across another soul whose Amygdala is permanently hijacked. He neither cares to correct himself nor feels sorry, let alone seeking any guidance from subordinates. He believes in being a bully so as to solicit unflinching (but unwilling) obedience; a rather cowardly step to secure his turf and feed his stained soul. Sure enough, people hate the sight of him walking in and are often found praying for him to get posted out. Perhaps, that's how the world is designed to function – a fine balance between positive and negative energies emitted by us humans. But I am sure you got my point.

Most humans develop a *false sense of complex* (*Inferiority or Superiority*) right from childhood. Blame it on our great game of gradings and ranks where in the *testimony of our self-worth is by means of a scribbled piece of certificate.* Have we ever seen a child or a school going kid go jubilant over his/ her friend's performance? *This is where the seeds of complex and jealousy are sown and how!* Fast forward some 20 years, the child (now an adult) carries the same into workplace and a rather catastrophic manifestation of this trait begins to take shape. This guy/gal now hesitates to ask for help as they're afraid of exposing their follies. *None of us want to be branded as troubled, do we?* Also, they hesitate in checking out on their friends' well-being on the pretext of *'He/she would have sought my help if required'.* Well, this very illusion or self-fulfilling prophecy has cost lives! (read suicides).

Friends and families are symbiotic and not symbolic. You can't do it all alone every single time. We must refrain from being lone wolves for our own good. It takes courage (NOT Compassion or Trust) to say *"Hey, I need your help"* or *"Hey, are you OK? I am worried about you".*

24 THE 3 FUNDAMENTAL 'TOOLS OF VERDICT'

A big(insincere) thanks to the ever-ballooning Social Media fuelled by its alter-ego, the technology, one of the greatest fears humans battle today is the **Fear of Judgement** and surprisingly, it's more pronounced on the social media. We are way too occupied in calibrating what we speak, do and post digitally based on the primal fear of being judged. ***Needless to say, we are spectacularly curating our social media profiles to portray ourselves to be summum bonums of a Good Life!*** Why wouldn't we when we ourselves are engaged in judging and passing verdicts on all and sundry round the clock? We need some serious rewiring to our gray maters here and how!

Albeit the very concept of judging others is itself laughable as it's almost everytime based on scanty knowledge of another person, yet I believe there are some fundamental questions which any sane human worth his salt would ask himself about another human he must deal with. Considering that by and large we basically deal and interact with three broad categories of individuals viz. ***Subordinates, Colleagues/ Friends*** and ***Superiors***, the fundamental verdict that these folks make about you revolves around the following questions ......

A Subordinate would ask – Is he a selfless Leader?

A Colleague/Friend would ask – Is he Helpful and Trustworthy?

A Superior would ask – Is he Truthful and an Asset?

I bet my last ten bucks in humbly arguing that our entire being fundamentally revolves around these questions and scoring a **'YES'** *in each of these is what makes anyone irrespective of his/ her profession, a spectacular human being – a rare commodity today indeed!* The irony today is that everyone sets out on their respective journeys with noblest of intentions but only few make it to the end unscathed while a vast majority fall prey to **Ethical Fading, Fame and Illusionary Success**.

Next time around you get itchy or tempted to judge another person based on trivial parameters (mostly fuelled by the Curated Social Media Profile), bite your tongue and use these 3 fundamental tools of verdict and make sure that you yourself score a 'YES' in all of them before even setting out to pass the verdict on others! The answers to these questions or tools will also help you to solve the most common conundrum plaguing any organisation today. We will explore that in next chapter.

25 THE LEADER-POLITICIAN CONUNDRUM

Every organisation (without exceptions) at every level has both Leaders and Politicians at helm. The term 'Neta' (Meaning politician in Hindi) is not just confined to politics. Considering the modus operandi of most Netas today, I prefer using it as a Metaphor of sorts to drive home a point. There is a thin-red-line between these two which often goes unnoticed. Let's fathom its subtlety through illustrations –

A Leader '**Inspires his Team**' to perform by '**Leading from Front**'.

A Neta '**Urges his Team**' for support through '**Lengthy Sermons**'.

A Leader has a '**Vision and Roadmap**' for his team and its members.

A Neta has a '**Personal Milestones Map**' for himself.

A Leader aims at '**Highest Professional Satisfaction**' for his team and no more!

A Neta aims at the '**Highest Possible Rank or Position**' for himself and no less!

A Leader is '**Genuinely Concerned**' about the welfare of his team members.

A Neta shows '**Symbolic Concern**' for the welfare of his team members.

A Leader '**Rebukes in Private but Praises in Public**' because he knows that *incentivising good behaviour will inspire everyone to work for the team.*

A Neta often '**Rebukes in Public but Praises in Private**' because he knows that *penalising bad behaviour will urge everyone to follow.*

A Leader sorts out '**What's wrong in the Team**' so that everyone feels 'happy and secured'.

A Neta sorts out '**Who's wrong in the Team**' so that everyone is scared and aware of consequences of disobedience.

A Leader doesn't take '**Yes**' or '**No**' for an answer without knowing '**Why**'.

A Neta doesn't take '**No**' for an answer and cares two hoots about '**Why**'.

A Leader generates '**Genuine Smiles**' out of inspiration as he walks in.

A Neta generates '**Simulated and Cosmetic Smiles**' out of desperation, anger, anxiety and fear as he walks in.

While both may deliver results, it's the Leader who will be remembered. How many do you remember? The funny part is that *you don't even know who you've been because none will confront you* (unless of course you go unreasonably haywire!). Leadership is a symbol of selflessness. *The Longer your Legacy lasts after you are no longer there, greater is the evidence that you have been Selfless in Leading your team.* Who do you choose to be? A decision on who you choose to be will dictate what kind of subordinates you rally around you. And that's a miniature version of how the world is handcrafted by the kind of human you choose to be.

26

THE POWER OF SPHERE OF INFLUENCE

Most of us would have heard the clichéd phrase *'Don't fret over things that are beyond your control'*. However, few of us take real cognizance of its intent. We, yet, often venture out into uncontrolled territories both physical and cognitive only to find ourselves wanting and disappointed. Let's apply some common sense (*not very common these days*) to fathom its true sense.

*Each of us, however big or small in our stature or position in our organisations have our own **Spheres of Influence** – A sphere within which your directions or instructions are implemented and in which you afford considerable latitude in the manner you lead your team. Why go far? Even a mother who is a homemaker has her own sphere of influence which includes her kids and spouse. It applies to all walks of life and not just our work places.*

A person can ensure *maximum efficiency through direct influence only within the said sphere of influence*. Anything beyond gets *uneconomical and disproportionate in effort vs. outcome analysis*. Because, that's the job of those under you as they have their own sphere! Venturing out beyond your own sphere is like *operating a 1000-mile screw driver helplessly and hoping for a change*. The point I am trying to make is simply this – ***If you ever feel the necessity of bringing about a change, do so within your sphere of influence and forget the rest!*** That's precisely why we have *hierarchical structures* literally across all domains, big and small alike. *It's laughable when a tea-shop owner comments on how the Modi Govt should operate in these challenging times of COVID but his own tea sucks!* That's because he is venturing beyond his sphere without influencing his own – *his shop workers and customers.* Similar analogy can be extrapolated to everyone. We see celebrities making philosophical comments about govt policies with little or no knowledge just because they have larger sphere of influence. You see, there is *no real difference between that tea-shop guy and such celebrities.*

If we all collectively make a resolution to positively impact our spheres of influence, the whole world will be transformed, isn't it? Why else would Mother Teresa make such a remark. ***So, what's your Sphere of Influence***?

We will now see what's the most important trait of a leader while engaging with his or her sphere of influence.

27 WALK THE TALK OR STAY SHUT!

We are all members of some team as part of some organisation irrespective of professions, isn't it? None of us is a lone warrior (or rather can't be), so to speak. Having said that, you would agree that **'Hypocrisy'** is the root cause of discontentment or lack of unison in any team. Let me convince you again. The moment a culture of **'Double Standards'** seeps in, the first seeds of a crackdown in the team's efficiency are sown. And like always, it's the leaders at the helm at every level who are blameworthy. **'Hypocrisy' or 'Double Standards' manifest when you don't 'Walk the Talk'.**

There are myriad instances to buttress this notion. For instance, *how motivated do you feel when your top political leadership urges you to maintain a strict lockdown while they themselves embark on an election rally? Why go macro? Consider a simple scenario of a family where in the father (the head or leader of his family) is a chain smoker. Can he expect his son not to lay his hands on a cigarette when the opportunity strikes?* Become the kind of leader that people would follow voluntarily, even if you had no title or position said Brian Tracy.

But, unless we establish a **rock-solid consistency between what we do and speak**, our teams won't strike a chord at all and we would end up **leading our teams more by default than by design**. I have seen a Second-in-Command who hauled up all and sundry by constantly monitoring weights of all ranks while handing out counselling and warning letters to obese personnel while he himself deprived a pregnant duck of her uniqueness. Sure enough, his words never made an iota of difference to the troops. Isn't the case similar in any organisation?

One of easiest jobs of leader at any level is to spell out his desires (or wish list) in a lengthy sermon – be it related to work ethics or integrity or morality or more commonly professed physical fitness or health today. However, the tougher part is to walk that talk! In other words, leading from front in anything you preach. Why else leaders like **Field Marshal Sam Maneckshaw** or **General Norman Schwarzkopf** from the Military and **Ratan Tata, Elon Musk, Steve Jobs, Jeff Bezos** or **Bill Gates** from the corporate are revered by all.*They are (or were) not just leaders but spellbinders of sorts who raise our spirits sky-high by every word they utter; They always walk the talk, don't they?*

In my humble view, if we can't walk the talk, we don't have the right to talk either! So, next time you talk, make sure you have the ability to walk! The leaders who walk the talk are microcosms of all thriving and successful organisations today. How micro and yet how influential are they? I will throw some interesting statistics up next to know that.

28 THE IDEAL 80/20 PRINCIPLE

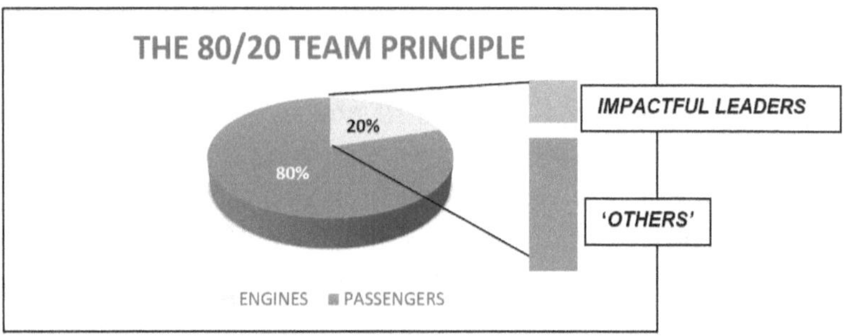

We all have heard of the famous **Pareto Principle** which states that *80% of the results are due to 20% of your efforts in a particluar area* and hence the need to prioritise and focus on the efforts that mattter and are impactful rather than grazing through the *'To-Dos'* or *'Checklists'* buffet-table indiscriminately. Many have even researched and applied this template to workplaces or organisations of any kind which means in any team, 80% of the productivity is due to efforts of only 20% of its players or employees. **It automatically means those handful of 20% shoulder 80% of responsibilities**. It's worth digging deep and knowing '**WHY**' lest knowing '**WHAT**' is of little consequence to our lives.

If you ask a bunch of 10 people, you will most likely get '***Competence'*** as an answer in majority as an explanation to this principle. However, may I humbly suggest, it's more to do with '***Attitude'*** than 'Competence'. Why else would there be phrases like '**You are hired for your skills but fired for your behaviour**'? Why else would famous Author and Speaker Shiv

Khera say '**There are more people in this world who are not working than those who are unemployed**' ? So much so for the principle and its root cause! Yet, I have made a courageous (read risky!) attempt to further deconstruct the 20% lot who are in the engine's seat of any team and how.

It's a no brainer that these 20% will rise very high in the hierarchy and will mostly be responsible for the overall growth of the organisation. However, a careful dissection of these 20% will reveal that 80% of them are purely concerned about rising to the top *'at all costs'* and no more! *They will be forgotten and despised the moment they step out of the team*. The balance 20% are the real-heroes or impact leaders. Ironically, these handful of men and women may not necessarily rise as high but *they will be adored, admired and emulated* by all and sundry because they are purely concerned about making an impact on their teams and its members *'at all costs'* and no more! They are the real bastions of selfless service that we so glibly profess in our conversations. In many ways, it's under these humble and impactful humans' blankets that most of *'others'* (the 80%) enjoy a healthy lifestyle and a wealthy bank balance.

Let's ask ourselves a simple yet soul-searching question – **'*Do I belong to the 80% or 20% or more genuinely 20% of 20%*** ? You now know the Ideal 80/20 principle ! There's another trait which separates these two kinds of humans. Let's find out next.

29 SUBTLETY BETWEEN OBEDIENCE AND YES-MANNNERS

> "A Yes-Man is a dangerous man. He is a Menace. He will go very far. He can become a Minister, a Secretary or a Field Marshal but he can never become a leader nor ever be respected. He will be used by his superiors, disliked by his colleagues and despised by his subordinates. So, discard the Yes-Man".
>
> – Field Marshal Sam Maneckshaw

Having interacted with my friends from all walks of life and professions, it was a no brainer to conclude that the single most decisive factor for an organisation's success is the **'Obedience of its Team Members'**. Yet, I was intrigued by the two terms – the conventional **'Obedience'** and the Colloquial **'Yes-Manship'** and wondered if they differ at all in meaning and intent. Many still believe they are synonymous and mere semantics. In essence, they are poles apart. Let's see how.

An Obedient Guy/Gal (famously known as **OG** in the Military) irrespective of profession does the right things every waking hour whether or not under watch or scrutiny. **They do so because their obedience is more towards**

their own deep rooted values and belief system which are omnipresent even in solitude. They do understand and appreciate that their bosses are transients in the 'Journey of Life' and thus are more dedicated towards the larger cause of their organisations and humanity than mere milestones of them or their higher-ups. They won't move a brick without establishing a fool-proof consistency with their own belief system with which they have bullet-proofed their minds against any 'lucrative wrongs'. *This is exactly why such souls are Man-Fridays wherever they are planted; true leaders can bet their last ten bucks on them blindly.*

On the other hand, a 'Yes-Man' has no such values or belief systems for he/she doesn't even believe they exist. **If at all, their only belief system is to fit-in with the larger crowd or their leader's aspirations (legitimate or illegitimate) nonchalantly because deep down they feel that's what accrues them maximum pay-offs in life**. Prima Facie, they are 'Pure Gold' for any leader but are catastrophic in the long run. They simply take the shape of the environment they are planted in like *water* with the terms **'Right Cause'** and **'Larger Good'** being mere semantics for them. Their sole purpose is to get ahead in life and show the world how successful they are; or so they think. **They define their Self-Worth with Net-Worth or their Title, little realising that they can't carry any baggage along with their own hearse**.

So, you see, that's the subtlety twixt the two. However, may I humbly confess *that the difference is so subtle that it's easy to overlook it, yet I feel it's so clear that it's impossible to mistake it*. The danger however lies in who you encourage because both the clans exist in any team. The clan you encourage most will be the most populous component in your team and hence dictate whether you have harnessed a **'Breed of Winners'** or a **'Bunch of Pleasers'**.

I always believe that your formative phase of schooling has a lot to do with shaping your character and personality. You see, it's easy to mould children into obedient souls if it is suitably inter-sprinkled in the training curricula of primary/preparatory/high schools. If such institutionalised measures are carefully *calibrated*, you may well end up harnessing a generation of sincere, hardworking and obedient citizens. But what happens when you don't *calibrate?* Let me share an interesting Analogy from Norman Dixon's 'Psychology of Military Incompetence' which can pretty much be a template for any organisation. It's about an era of 1930s when a typical English Preparatory School institutionalised authoritarian *'Bowel-Training'.* Yes, you read that right. The Headmaster's wife would make daily entries of every student in her register to include a 'YES' or a 'NO' for successful or unsuccessful ablutions respectively. Boys who said 'NO' on return were given doses of castor oil and liquid cascara to make it a 'YES' which wasn't a pleasant experience for the kid by any measure. You don't need a psychologist to appreciate how it was a perfect recipe for handcrafting a generation of 'YES-MEN'. And if it was happening in such a systematic manner in 1930s, there is little reason to believe that it wasn't a product of decades of such brainwashing prior to it. Many of my friends and seniors who I consider to be atleast ten times as worldly wise as me opine that this very culture of 'Yes-Manship' is a direct by product of centuries of British-Raj in many countries. Especially India. It's hard to disagree with them, isn't it?

Whichever organisation you belong to, make a list of your subordinates under two broad categories of *'Obedient Souls'* and *'Yes-Men'* (of course, it includes women as well). The single most honourable deed for you as a leader would be to populate the former and dry up the latter. You will be amazed to see how cheerful, innovative, motivated and successful your team suddenly manifests into.

Reality Check

[List out individuals in your team in the undermentioned categories:]

OBEDIENT SOULS	YES-MEN

30 THE POWER OF 'PAT ON THE BACK'

Anyone who is in his/her late 20s and beyond and has a decent job for a living would by now have realised that **Maturity, Competence and Kindness doesn't necessarily manifest with age and experience.** It doesn't atleast by default, so to speak. Having said that, in today's era which is flooded by *young and energetic entrepreneurs* who rose from rags to riches *without any lineage roll-overs* or by **Military men and women** who are *not necessarily 2nd generation*, there is little denying the fact that age is a mere number.

Even a 60-year-old can be inspired by the talent, hardwork, dedication and kindness of a 20-year-old. Mind you, the former was well settled in life while the latter was conceived in the womb. Even I have been unimaginably inspired by many young kids who are just past their teenage. This auto-reinforces the fact that *in any organisation, the movers and shakers are the younger lot who have just embedded themselves into the rut of it all!* However, statistics projected tell a different story. It's worth knowing why….

I have already dwelled upon a little on this aspect in the chapter on selflessness. But digging deep won't hurt, will it?

We think way too much before saying 'Well-Done' or 'Thank You' to our subordinates. Even if someone impresses by his/her dedication and output, most leaders often give a calibrated response or accolades. And as the famous author *Liz Uram* alludes to in one of her books, *many leaders fear that the subordinates will 'Grow out of their Boots'and exude arrogance if praised too much.* I wonder who can't relate to this!

One of the surveys indicates that a simple '**Pat on the Back**' increases your efficiency by **85**%. While this statistic might sound crazy, haven't you felt the same at your work places? The converse is uncomfortably true when you don't get the required recognition. *It takes greater courage to look into your subordinates' or loved ones' eyes and say '**Well-Done/Thank You**', '**I am Proud of You**' than giving orders or instructions.* However, as we will see in the next chapter, most of the leaders' ability (or inability) to praise their subordinates is punctuated by a very tricky dilemma.

31 THE DILEMMA OF PERFORMANCE VS BEHAVIOUR

> **"Leadership is a potent combination of Strategy and Character.**
> **But if you must be without one, be without strategy".**
>
> **– Gen Norman Schwarzkopf**

I recently happened to interact on a conference call with three of my friends all of who were from three very different professions (Software, Law and Banking). An interesting similarity accidently came to light. All these organisations heavily incentivised performance but never the behaviour (ethical or unethical). In other words, their 'Ends' were more important than 'Ways' or 'Means'. *A subtle way of saying 'Hook or Crook'!* Of course, any profit driven organisation would base its agenda on this very premise. But I wonder if it's healthy or worthy for any organisation in the long run.

A harsh truth we all must come to terms is that we mostly incentivise performance irrespective of the behaviour adopted towards it unless some riff-raff accidently gets unearthed! *This stems straight from our own ill-conceived concept of success – **More money, higher position or ranks, higher academic pursuits.*** We want quick fixes in anything and everything we do which is why most of us get hijacked by the 'Hook or Crook' narrative. In reality, this is an illusion because *any performance through ethical behaviour is a hustle which very few are willing to undergo.* And understandably, there are no quick fixes. You will fall short many times but in the longer run, you would have evolved to unimaginable proportions much to the surprise (and envy) of 'Quick-Fixers'. This is exactly why chasing success makes us myopic and self-centred. You always see the quick-fixers professing that honesty, integrity and character are all crap and are subject to opportunities, don't you? You won't be the Man-Friday of your leaders in any case (unless they share the same wavelength as you which is a tsunami in making!) Why else would Gen Schwarzkopf make such a statement? (read quote above).

Irrespective of any profession, incentivising ethical behaviour (with or without performance) has far reaching consequences for any organisation and will definitely leave a legacy for others to emulate for centuries ahead. As leaders at any level, it's our moral obligation to intimately understand the path chosen by our subordinates to accomplish a task and be more concerned about the ways and means than ends. Because, **no matter how spectacular are your ends, you will always be defined by the ways and means you adopted to achieve those ends.** It's not uncommon to find folks at your work places who hit the target every single time before the deadline much to the amusement of their bosses but resort to 'hook or crook' mantra while accomplishing them.

A surest way of ensuring ethically driven performances is to spell out categorically to your team as to what's acceptable to you and what's not, no matter what's the ultimate output. Before spelling out, you need to make a note of every goal or end state you want your team to achieve and what are the behaviours desired there in. The following model will help:-

End State or Goal	Desirable Behaviour(s)	Undesirable Behaviour(s)
1.		
2.		
3.		
4.		
5.		
6.		

We shall now see another aspect closely related to the behaviour of your team members and why it's catastrophic when misinterpreted.

32 SINCERITY AND AMBITION: A COUNTERINTUITIVE STANCE

It's not uncommon in any workplace to brand sincere and hardworking employees as *Ambitious* even to the extent of propagating a sense of dislike or hatred about them in the environment. It is worth realising why this practice by most of us causes an invisible damage to any organisation which at times may become irreparable in the long run both for the individual and as well as for the organisation.

I firmly believe that if an individual's ambitious attitude, be it a desire to rise high in hierarchy or earn more money, are based on the foundation of sincerity and self-respect, they are bound to uplift any organisation's performance. The problem arises when this isn't the case. Haven't we seen people who work with extra exuberance only when under observation and palm it off to others if the stakes ain't high? These people have ambitions based on the foundation of *transactional attitude* who will give an input only for as long as there is an out-of-proportion output. They don't hesitate to play the blame game when cornered and play victims every waking hour to secure their reputation. Thus, they can never become an asset to any organisation as their sole agenda is to populate their own personal asset column. Yet, it's such an irony that most organisations fail to recognise the same because the short term gains they offer are humungous, often obscuring you from the long-term reality.

As leaders in any organisation, it is our moral obligation to identify and realise this malaise at hand. Another interesting (and appalling) feature of hierarchical organisations is that of *Appraisals* and *Confidential Reports*. The present system has a top-down model which means your ascent is primarily dictated by the reports given by your superiors. This very system is exploited by the so-called transactional leaders; the ones with wrong foundations. **Be it any organisation, you will see plenty of them around who are Man-Fridays for their bosses but are autocrats for their subordinates.** What good is it to lead a vexed team when hardly any of those below you subscribe to your work-ethics but you keep rising high because you just seem to crack the code of *'Work where Visible'* and *'Impress those who Matter'* so very well. And more importantly, what good is it for the organisation or your team as whole to have such souls who have but one agenda in their lives – *'Ascent at all Costs'.* Takes my mind back to the illustration of *Personal Anger Management* where in you spit out your anger selectively at folks who are least equipped to hurt you back! I really don't know how it will change. I really don't know how will the bosses device practices or institutionalise procedures to know the worth of an individual through the lens of his subordinates. But change, it must. We ought to encourage and incentivise the former while discouraging the latter. Apply this template to any organisation of any size and level, it's exponential growth is inevitable.

Well, there's another vital ingredient of an impactful leader without which literally every positive attribute you possess may prove counter-productive. Which is why it's a big deal. Let's discover next.

33 STAYING HUMBLE IS A BIG DEAL!

> **"Humility is not thinking less of yourself, it's thinking of yourself less".**
>
> **– C.S Lewis**

We humans by evolutionary history are competitive, insecure and predatory often fuelled by mammoth egos and self-centric dealings. Yet, we find some handful of souls who are humble and down-to-earth inspite of whatever they have achieved, materialistically and professionally alike. This handful lot, I am told is only 5% of the entire world's population! Why is it a big deal ? Why only few of us choose to be humble? What's in it or isn't that we make the choice of being or not being? *In my humble view, 'Success' is the culprit!*

Being successful in any sphere of life *naturally* injects a subconscious ego into our veins. The definition of success is a bit twisted here. This success can be in terms of any edge we enjoy over others and not necessarily academic or professional in nature. It can be as simple as having more friends, more wealth, better looks (Yes! You read that right), better communication skills or more commonly perceived, better professional success. Our inflated egos then start dictating our conversations, friendships and priorities in life. We often start dealing with similarly equipped individuals and thus become transactional in nature. And soon enough, the clichéd expression of *'Success Getting into Your Head'* manifests in your *Grey Matter. All of this is passive and subconscious and happens to all of us unless we actively and consciously combat it.* Yes, that's a default mode in humans. If you haven't done anything about it, the environment will tell you in more ways than one that you ain't humble.

That's exactly what those 5% of humans do. They *practice* humility day in and out. It seldom comes naturally. And as *practice makes you perfect,* they have become perfectly humble humans on earth today. So, you see, it's a big deal! A simple way to practice humility is to pass a gentle and genuine smile every time you greet a person, going out-of-way to help someone in need or seek your help and inspire everyone around you by your simplicity. The other day, I watched an award function on TV where in a few famous singers were being bestowed with *Best Performances* awards. There were two singers who got the awards, who I would like to name as A and B (keeping their identities discreet). Here are their words to the audience on receiving their respective awards –

Singer A – *"My fans want to know what's it like for me to not win an award. They will never know".*

Singer B – *"Thank you all my fans and support staff. We artists thrive on your support and even an iota of this appreciation couldn't have been possible without you".*

Hands on heart, who do you think is more humble here.

Success is an Opium. Where you draw it into dictates who you are. Draw it into your heads and you will belong to the 95% majority. Let your humble heart do the talking and you will never cease to succeed, because nothing is permanent. *Success is but a rented asset and the rent is due every day!* An important and out of proportion fall out of humility is the ability to handle a funny thing called *Criticism.* Let's see how in next chapter.

34 HANDLE THIS FUNNY THING WITH CARE!

Criticism is a funny thing! It can annoy or displease even the most open-minded people who always welcome critiques. Though many people seek criticism or critique, hands-on-heart, most are not welcoming to your representations or observations either. Being open to criticism is more of a symbolism these days. So, are all criticisms bad? or rather should all criticisms be shelved or accepted? It's worth pondering.

There are two kinds of people who criticise. *One set of people criticise out of genuine concerns for your growth and improvement and the other set simply criticise for pleasure.* For most of us, parents, spouses and a few selected friends, relatives and seniors fall in the first category. The second set of folks criticise for fun or pleasure. They often criticise anything and everything that comes their way, be it people, organisations or systems at large. They do this primarily to prove that they are *Good Humans (read misfits)* stuck on an unkind planet. While the former category always cares for you, the latter care for none but themselves and hence keep blaming the entire universe as a cover up for their follies. *Close your eyes and try relating people in each category – their faces will start flashing back and forth in your mind, won't they?*

An effective way to deal with this *funny thing* is to criticise only those who you really care about (and NOT for pleasure) and ignore all *critiques of pleasure that come your way!* And this is one of the greatest manifestations of humility that we saw in the previous chapter. If criticising someone gives you as much pain as themselves, you have every right to criticise. Only then can this funny thing be used to give a fillip to our growth.

A very disturbing manifestation of criticism these days is sarcasm. Far from being funny, it doesn't inspire even an iota of confidence even if it's through good will. Rather, is it a good will at all? We will find out.

SARCASM OUT OF *GOOD WILL* IS *ILL WILL*

It is not uncommon to find people finding solace out of passing sarcastic remarks on others! And surprisingly, some do it so very consistently that often their true statements are misunderstood and their true self-worth never understood.

Many profess that they use this as a tool to motivate their peers or subordinates in the hope that they will take it as a challenge and prove them wrong. Sure, some might, but many others won't; infact, never!

Well, that's not even the point. Whether or not your target audience gets benefitted by your self-styled sarcasm, it never does any good to your personal reputation or image, so to speak. *I am yet to see a leader or a person being genuinely loved or adored for their sarcasm.*

Consider these instances....

I have seen a person very senior in position or chair passing remarks to an obese guy that *'you can survive for weeks without food as you have adequate reserve'* in your tummy, oblivious of the fact that the poor guy was battling *thyroid*. Another person was seen downplaying a subordinate's idea saying that *'you constantly surprise me with your dumbness'*. Want more? How about a person passing a remark – *'I am sorry if I hurt your feelings when I called you stupid. I really thought you already knew'*. How inspiring are these remarks to you? I am sure there are multitude of ways and means to inspire people around you. When the very literal meaning of sarcasm means *'mocking'*, there is little evidence to prove that it can be of *'Good Will'*. And surprisingly, it harms both the originator and the target audience. *As leaders, if there is one trait that we should all consciously try not to fall prey, it is this because.........*

Sarcasm is always out of ill will!

36 BE CAREFUL WHAT YOU ASK FOR!

The concept of *Leadership* has intrigued humans since time immemorial. There are tons of research being carried out even as I write this, aiming at *'digging deep'* and *'knowing it all'* about what it takes to be an effective and a fail-proof leader. *Yet, the complexity of it unravels each day, multitude of its manifestations, each with its own unique 'Code of Ethics' specific to an organisation.* **I dare say, there isn't one human being on planet earth who can beat his chest hollow and declare *'I Know It All'* about Leadership including those who have authored books on it.**

That notwithstanding, there are numerous traits of a leader that cut across every organisation which inevitably become sine qua non for making an effective 'Team Captain'. *Being compassionate, empathetic, learned (scholar) and having an attitude of selflessness and tolerance for ambiguity are but a few to name.* However, in my humble view, there are three traits which become *Super Non-Negotiable* if you truly want to be an impactful leader of your team and want your team to win. The Three pillars are – **Moral Values**, **Ethical Behaviour** and **an Aversion to Free Lunches.** *Go check out any hierarchical set up of any team, it's leaders with these traits that are most admired, adored and respected. Professional skills take a back seat which is exactly what the quote by Gen Schwarzkopf in chapter 31 tries to buttress.*

As leaders at any level, we may be dressed like a Gentleman in front of our subordinates or team members but without these 3 traits, we are stripped naked. **The world, past**

and present is replete with examples of such leaders who are professionally super humans but are *'Morally Naked'*.

*It's our moral obligation (again, if we truly want to be effective leaders) to **'NOT ASK'** for an unreasonable favour or job or task or give orders to that effect, which our subordinates can't refuse out of obedience but if refused, can piss us off.* It takes courage and heart to come to terms with the fact that when we ask or give such orders or seek such targets borne out of utter disregard to these 3 traits, **90%** of them don't say **'NO'** due to their own aspirational dreams (and it's completely OK) but a **100 %** of them are **'Unwilling'** deep inside. Be careful what you ask for if you want to 'Lead'.

As we now near the end of the process of deconstruction of leadership, it's important to analyse whether there is a most effective language at all, for a leader to be most effective and inspiring.

37 A MYTH CALLED SPOKEN ENGLISH

Most of us Indians are quick to declare someone to be professionally sound, intellectual and polished merely because he/she speaks flamboyant and fluent English. We laugh it out and even make fun of people whose mother-tongue effect creeps into their accents – be it Punjabis, Haryanvis, South-Indians or North-Eastern folks and also proudly brand them as being 'desi' or 'not so intellectual'. This idiotic and foolish attitude of us cuts across all professions – Corporate, Military, Medical and multitude of others. Well, that's not without concrete historical reasons. It's the case with every single nation that has ever been colonised by the Britishers. We will have to rewind our clocks back by a couple of centuries to know its roots. To know why we behave the way we behave! This is an important issue to be understood because many organisations today have been foolishly hyphenating English with intellect and leadership skills. Back in 19th century, when the Britishers had fairly stabilised their grip in the sub-continent, a necessity was felt, of creating a a class of interpreters between the masses and the government. Apart from many other reasons, the multi-lingual Indian ecosystem was the primary argument for such a policy. It might come as a surprise to know that English as a literature wasn't taught anywhere else in the world then. Thus, it was *invented* in India, for India, for the purpose of furthering their own interests and ensuring a smooth-run for the colonisers. Professor Gauri Vishwanathan, in her thesis titled 'Mask of Conquest' categorically alludes to all of the aforesaid stances further buttressing the motive of introducing

English Literature into the Indian society. It was more about colonizing the minds of Indian masses than about bringing about any educational renaissance. This not only let English literature make inroads into our education curriculums but also ensured its infiltration into our grey matters. So much so that, it's almost undesirable to have someone around who doesn't *utter good English*. Take a look at few of the excerpts from the infamous speech of Lord Babington Macaulay in the early 19th Century –

"No reader of English literature can deny that a single shelf of good European library was worth the whole native literature of India and Arabia".

"It is no exaggeration to say, that all historical information which has been collected from all the books written in Sanskrit language is less valuable than what may be found in most paltry abridgements of preparatory schools in England".

"We need people who are Indian in *Blood* and *Colour* but English in *Tastes*, *Opinions*, *Morals* and *Intellect*".

Rightly evinced by Gauri, implementation of New Education system leaves those who are colonized with a limited sense of their past. It makes them see their past as one wasteland of non-achievement and it makes them want to distance themselves from that wasteland. Not only does colonial education eventually create a desire to dissociate with native heritage, but it affects the individual and the self-confidence and in many many ways, his/her self-esteem. Tell me, as an Indian, if you haven't felt this!

Fast forward to today, aren't we the biggest hypocrites and racists on planet earth when we, on one hand, want the Brits to apologize for their atrocities but on the other have clung to their language like leeches so much so that not knowing good English can cost you your living in India? It's time we de-hyphenate 'communication skills' from this predatory language. We collectively need some intense and genuine soul-searching here! Two of the most powerful and developed nations in the world today are in our own Asian continent. Do they officially speak English? You have your answers!

An organisation only needs leaders who can communicate well with their team or subordinates and inspire them to chase goals and achieve what they dreamt of. Does it always merit a Good English? I have my serious doubts! That's not to downplay the humungous opportunities this language has on offer. Why else would I have penned this book in English! It's just way far reaching than any other language today. But it won't hurt to know the root cause of it, does it?

38 EMPATHY IS A *FEELING* AND NOT A *CONCEPT*

> "Leadership is about empathy. It is about having the ability to relate to and connect with people for the purpose of inspiring and empowering their lives".
>
> – Oprah Winfrey

In my humble view, the term 'Empathy' is overrated in its *conception* but falls way short of expectations in *execution*. There are many leadership experts, eminent celebrities and even military bigwigs who profess the concept of empathy as an effective tool of leading a *'Happy Team'*. However, little do we realise that it's more than just a concept. It's a *'Feeling'*. And unless that feeling seeps into your grey matter and hits all your body cells, it will remain a concept and no more. **It's no rocket-science to realise that whatever is conceptual, almost certainly never reaches the desired degree of execution.**

A fool-proof way of developing empathy for your subordinates at any level is to go through the same routine hardships as them which invariably injects the *'feelings'.* Military follows it to this day. *An Officer stays in the barracks of his soldiers for the first month of his commissioned service roughing it day in and out with those who will march on his orders into jaws of death unquestioned.* Hence, you will always see military folks exhibiting extraordinary levels of empathy even if they are dealing with a civilian (well, that is not to say there aren't exceptions!). While this kind of an arrangement is not feasible across all organisations, what I am suggesting with great love and respect is this – ***You got to feel (literally feel) what every member of your team feels. It's as if a part of you resides in every body cell of your subordinates.***

For instance, if you want to develop empathy for a waiter at a restaurant, you got to feel (literally feel) how his typical day unfolds, what he goes through and how he manages being the sole bread-winner of his family. Because if you don't, it's more likely that you will admonish him for getting your ordered cuisine late.

If you want to develop empathy for any subordinate of your team, you got to feel (literally feel) and imagine what is his/ her present work-load, how is he/she doing on family front and how cheerful he/she has been of late. Because if you don't, it's more likely that you will admonish him/her for not completing your task in time (which you thought, sitting in your cosy air-conditioned office, to be the only task he/she had in the day!)

I can't stress this enough. Empathy is a Feeling and NOT a Concept. The more it is professed as a concept, less are the chances of its manifestation on ground. Next time around, you feel like showering bile on someone, close your eyes and actively inject the *Feeling!*

I will now buttress my view on empathy by taking an aid of how most of us have been fooled for ages about the concept of stress.

39 HOW YOU (AND ME) WERE FOOLED ABOUT STRESS

The concept of stress has intrigued me since ages. Of all other curiosities that kept me scratching my mediocre brain, one thing stood apart – *What's the relation between the levels of stress and the position you hold in any hierarchical setup?*

I have come to realise that one of the most misconstrued concepts of stress is the notion that in any given organisational set up, the level of stress increases manifold as you climb the ladder. In 1950s, a famous experiment was conducted to substantiate the same which came to be known as '**The Executive Stress Syndrome**'. Famous Neuroscientist *Joseph Brady* gathered a bunch of **Rhesus Monkeys** (Yes, you read that right!). *One group was subjected to an electric shock every 20 seconds for 6 hours. The other group, labelled as so called '**Executive Monkeys**' were subjected to similar jolts except that they had a lever nearby which they could press to prevent the shocks which they ultimately discovered by mischievously fiddling around.* Strangely, the executive monkeys with greater control started dropping dead from stomach ulcers. Lo and Behold, the Executive stress syndrome was born! The thematic premise built from thereon was that even though the *executive monkeys* have greater control, the fact that they have to make decisions takes a toll on their cognitive bandwidth and hence, they feel stressed.

What's laughable about this experiment is (which of course was debunked by tons of other researches that followed) our failure to realise two aspects – One, Stress management is more a function of both quantum and the ability to cope and not just the former and two, we ain't monkeys! I don't say this without backing. To get a much broader view and base my stance about stress through a larger canvas of facts and ground realities, I spoke with a host of professionals from various backgrounds viz. corporate, Military (I didn't have to speak to anyone though), Medical and Entrepreneurs. Let me walk you through what I could distil about the degree of control we all have as we climb the ladder of, I hate to say it though, rat race. For simplicity sake, I have divided individuals (employees and bosses included) into three broad categories.

Aspect	Degree of control		
	Intern/Young Employee/ Fresher/ Soldier	**Mid-Level Management and Leadership Positions**	**Bosses (at all levels)**
Waking up in the morning	Lowest	Medium	Highest
Reaching Office	Lowest	Medium	Highest
Intense Physical and Mental Work Load	Lowest	Medium	Highest
Flexibility of Postponing Tasks	Lowest	Medium	Highest
Affordability of taking a day off at random	Lowest	Medium	Highest
Supervisory layers above and their frequency of screwing your mind by breathing down your neck	Lowest	Medium	Highest

As you can glean from the above, a CEO or leader at any level has far more flexibility to postpone or selectively deal with *stress-bombs* as compared to an intern who has all and sundry breathing down his/her neck 24x7. What matters is the *Resultant Stress* which is the product of *Quantum of Stress* and the *Ability to Cope*. Have a look at this model:-

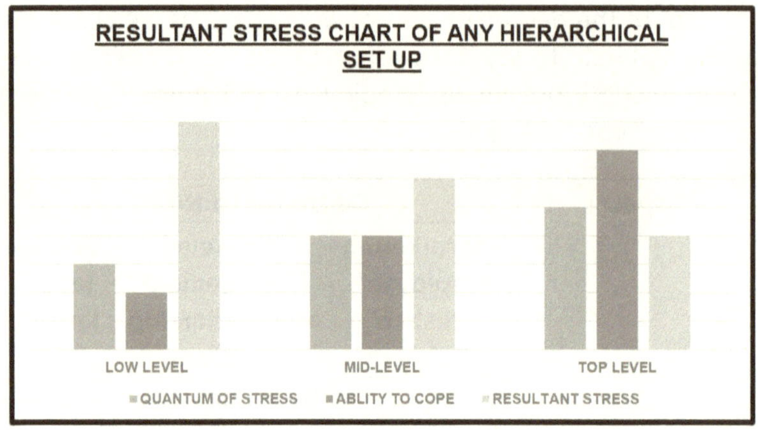

As we rise higher, our ability to cope with stress increases disproportionately vis-a-vis its quantum. Thus, the resultant stress is much lower.

It's our moral obligation in any hierarchical set up to be kind, considerate and empathetic towards the lower-rung employees who are just born in the team and are in the process of solving the jigsaw puzzle of work-life balance and whose quota of stress (read *resultant stress*) is unfathomably high.

As we close this segment of deconstruction of True Leadership, I offer you a prayer which shall help you to wade through waves of uncertainty and bursts of disillusionment to which most of us commonly fall prey to. I call it a prayer of Selfless Leader.

THE PRAYER OF A SELFLESS LEADER

When it pains to see many around you Eying for Awards Galore,
May God give you strength to realise you're here to Inspire and No More.

When your heart aches to see people obsessed with 'Carrot and Stick',
May God give you heart to reinforce that you're Sane and they're Sick.

When it frustrates to see leaders go gaga over Perks and Privileges,
May God give you clarity to know Frugality is how you'll be worshipped for Ages.

When you're disturbed to see people Addicted to Free Lunches,
May God give you perspective that 'It's all mysteriously taken back' often in Big Bunches.

When it hurts to hear people say 'Morals and Ethics' are mere 'Lack of Opportunity',
May God give you sanity to realise you'll be known for your Character and Not Competence and that that knowledge stays for posterity.

When it perturbs to see bosses using subordinates as a stepping stone,
May God reinforce your belief that such souls will forever be disobeyed in Combat Zone.

When people profess that being Unambitious is being Careless, May God give you confidence that you're doing fine and courage to say 'I Couldn't Care Less'.

When it frustrates to see your Obedience being taken for granted, May God give you maturity to navigate coz you're not meant to decay but To Bloom Where Planted.

When it pains to see many around you Eying for Awards Galore, May God give you strength to realise you're here to Inspire and No More.

You are here to Inspire and No More.......

PART III

FUEL YOUR GROWTH

Having reset your minds to factory settings and understood the value of True Leadership, it's important for us to use it to give a fillip to our growth and lead a happy and successful teams wherever we are planted. Everyone wants to be rich and famous, influential, successful and be at their personal best (and often beat even that benchmark) for as long as they are alive and kicking. While all of us know *'What we Want',* few have fathomed *'What it Takes'* and have actually embarked on a mission to realise them. Those very few and I am hopeful you will eventually be one of them too, perhaps realise that if you want to stand where you are, you must run; But run a race of your own and not the race (read rat race) the world prescribes to you for only then will you be ever influential and impactful till you hit the grave. An important aspect of your personal growth is to have a *Game Plan* or a *Dream* which must be big enough on conception to scare others (and perhaps you too) but small enough to start to encourage you to embrace and continue. And that's where will kick start our last segment.

41 DREAM BIG, START SMALL

Setting Giant Goals and going full throttle from day 1 is an assured recipe of disaster. It's not uncommon to see most of us set ambitious targets and go berserk from the word *'GO'*, only to see our own concept falling flat on its face as we soon fizzle out. There is a deep routed cause for such tendencies by most people today. We humans have the innate desire of achieving overnight success or atleast quicker success, so to say. We are never, ever patient with the process and instead keep dreaming about the *desired end state* day in and out. This is further substantiated by the fact that *we detest pain and savour pleasure*. Why else would binge watching movies on *'NETFLIX'* (a symbolic illustration) give you phenomenal amounts of joy while even a thought of reading or exercising or any other pursuits we have been long procrastinating about, give you stress and discomfort?

The best way to tackle this is to *'Start Small'*. Say, your goal is to develop abs. Most of us turn into beast mode on day 1 and work out for one hour, only to find ourselves lacking the courage to repeat it all over the next day. Instead, you could work out for only 10 minutes! Never mind the output. This gives you an assurance that it isn't difficult (read painful) to repeat it again. Likewise, if you want to cultivate a reading habit, it's foolish to read 40-50 pages on day 1 as if you are at a *Gun-Point* ordered to finish the day's quota! Even a page or two will do the trick. This template could be applied literally to any goal we are chasing today. A fascinating thing about starting small is that when you *stack these small starts over a period of a week or a fortnight*, you won't need willpower to increase or intensify your efforts further and soon you will begin to derive pleasure, purely out of satisfaction unlike 'NETFLIX' which is out of pure laze! It's such a key to *Dream Big but Start Small*. But before even you take those baby steps, it's important to realise one harsh truth about Growth and Success. The truth which at times made me laugh at myself and many of my Gen Z buds.

42 FUNNY TRUTH ABOUT GROWTH AND SUCCESS

We are unimaginably blessed to live in this age. Thanks to the ballooning Information and Technology fuelled ferociously by social media, it's hard to think beyond YouTube and Google when it comes to finding solutions to *'Anything'* we are confronted with today. Yes, Anything and Everything, if I may add. Yet, allow me to make an interesting (and funny) psychological revelation of us humans and our mindsets. Look at the few YouTube videos and Google links I came across while I searched for solutions for my quota of *'Anythings'*.......

Quickest and Easiest way to get 6 pack abs.

Loose stubborn belly fat in 7 days.

Write and Publish your book in just 30 days.

From Amateur to Author in 20 days.

How to speak fluent English in 7 days.

5 Simple steps to quit smoking.

Become a millionaire just by waking up early.

The aforesaid taglines are not chosen incidentally or carelessly. They are targeting the funny, yet intriguingly fascinating aspect of *Most Human Brains* (there's a reason why I use *'Most'* here!). **Most of us want Growth and Success real bad but also want it to be super-nice and easy and above all, want it real quick.** Atleast to begin with. Replace some of these titles to say, *'6 pack abs in 18 months'* or *'Learn flawless English in 20 months'* or *'Author's 12 week workshop'* and you will know why you won't even click on the link to know how (even if it actually takes that long to manifest).

The point I am trying to make is this – **real Growth and Success is Hard. And Painful. And Messy. And full of Sacrifices. And full of ups and downs, if I dare add!** More importantly, it demands a truck load of time and more! This harsh truth perfectly explains why most of those wanting it to be 'Easy' fizzle out the moment first drops of uneasy sweat trickle down their comfy faces. Because, it's so counterintuitive to what the YouTube or Google promised through those money-minting bloggers! Real winners *'Know it All'* before they *'Endure it All'*.

How willing are you to embrace **REAL GROWTH** vs. **EASY GROWTH**?

I will now walk you through a habit which, if embraced, is going to completely change your life. It certainly did change mine.

43 RISE EARLY, RULE THE ROOST

Of all the Good Habits that I have cultivated over the years, if there's one habit that I will be most proud of is this – *Rising Early*. And believe you me, it has the potential to transform your productivity and impact manifold and above all help you grow and perform at your personal best at a rather exponential pace. I have handcrafted this little chapter out of genuine concern for those who want to **Operate by Design and NOT by Default** but are somehow in a fix as to where to start. If you are ever looking at a *Self-Overhaul in terms of habits and rituals to make you super-productive and efficient, I say this again, let this be the first nut to crack – **Wake Up Early**. If you start your day by design, there are more chances that you will end it by design too. There are tons of research and books to buttress this view and each is an eye-opener to say the least. But don't take my word for it. I will dissect this concept which is part scientific and part philosophical.

Spirituality has it that the time between 4 am to 5:30 am is called '**Brahma Mahurta**' or '**The Creator's Time**' which essentially is about *90 minutes before sunrise*. During this phase, our mind and body are *most receptive to the* *positive cosmic energies which augment our creativity, IQ and productivity.* This is also the time during which we can easily access the **Subconscious Mind** (that drives behaviour) and the **Limbic Brain** (that affects memory) which is why our elders urged us to study early in the morning rather than late at night. And we all detested it as kids, didn't we? Another important aspect of this duration is that the kind of **Tranquillity** observed in this phase will never be same during the day as you get engrossed in the chaos and rat-race.

Scientifically, it is said that release of **'Cortisol'**, the fear hormone is maximum in the morning which is why we dread waking up and keep hitting the snooze button. Waking up early beats this and makes you much braver during the day and alleviates self-doubt. **'Dopamine'** is a pleasure neurotransmitter which is released on doing things we are obsessed with which is why you keep sifting through your smartphone whole day. It's rather a corollary of sorts because sifting through our smartphones releases dopamine which gets you obsessed with it. Haven't we all added about 10 items to our Amazon cart and went on to casually place an order for 8 of them not because we needed them urgently but because we feel happy when *'New Stuff'* gets delivered? That's dopamine doing the trick. The impact of e-marketing on our lives cant be gainsaid for it has brought all our needs literally to our doorsteps. We, however, don't realise, it also brings along a complimentary commodity (dopamine) with it. This is the basis of all addiction – Good or Bad. Back to our topic of rising early, waking up early associates it with dopamine which is best utilised for a productive habit. Amongst many others are **'Serotonin'** and **'Oxytocin'** which elevate our **Moods**, **Kindness**, **Compassion** and **Love** making you *less irritable during the day.*

If such amazing are its payoffs, do you still want to lie on bed during this hour? This applies to all and sundry who want to make it count. You could be a *wanna be artist, an actor, a businessman, a start-up guy/gal, an engineer, doctor or a solider.* The list is limited only by imagination. This is the time for boosting your efficiency and creativity thereby making a difference wherever you are planted. *I can bet my last ten bucks that it will transform you as you will be amazed at how productive and creative is our brain if given the right ecosystem.* An amazing payoff of locking into this habit of rising early is that it's a doorway to embrace a plethora of micro habits which we always want to, but don't find time for. It could range anything from exercising to reading to singing to playing a Guitar to Meditating. It also enables to set aside some Chaos-Free time to do disruptive thinking that will be a needle mover for your organisation or your family. The list is literally endless. Many of my friends and relatives have latched on to this habit on my humble advice and they can't say enough how it has given them a second-life. But don't take my word for it. Embrace it to believe it. *Rise Early, Rule the Roost!* We will now learn about another habit which, most people, like me, wish they were educated about decades ago!

THE SINGLE MOST LIFE-CHANGING HABIT

> **"If we encounter a man of rare intellect, we should ask him what books he reads".**
>
> **– Ralph Waldo Emerson**

Open the YouTube and it's not hard to find videos with thumbnails that read *"Five things I wish I knew when I was 20"*; *"I wish I was told this when I was 20"*; It could well be marketing tactics though, as these phrases are cognitively magnetic and subconsciously guide your fingers on the *'Click Button'*, if there's really one habit which I genuinely wish someone had told me about or I rather daresay, forced me into it, it's this – **Reading**! So huge are its payoff that I wish somebody had shoved it down my throat forcefully. I would have thanked that person till eternity. Of course, your regrets are justified when you start at the age of 31, aren't they?

Reading is like having *one on one conversation with the authors who by virtue of their enormous experience and talents enable us navigate through uncertain times like a torchlight of knowledge and a compass of wisdom*. It's hard not to agree that our educational system by and large (more so at the elementary school level) is flawed to a great extent which encourages *rote learning* with little effort towards developing an *analytical mind*. Imagine how better learned our future generation would be if every school going kid is made (read forced!) to read at least one book of suitable genre in a month or a quarter. This may well be part of the curriculum so to speak. Having said that, yet, choosing what to read has a profound influence on your productivity and efficiency. If I were to pick three genres which must form part of every wanna be reader's inventory, they are these – **Self-help**, **Leadership** and **History** (of your respective professions).

Self-Help books offer so much of an insight into our personality development repertoire that it can transform you in no time. Building good habits, developing willpower, gratitude and mastering your domain are but a few payoffs accrued.

Leadership is an omnipresent trait transcending through history of mankind and cutting across every profession today. Reading about it helps us to continuously and consciously sharpen our knives to stay relevant, be counted, be impactful and lead our teams well.

Reading about history gives us a perspective as to how the world has evolved and what lessons can be learnt. For instance, a uniformed soldier must read about military history which enables him to avoid fighting the next war like the last. An entrepreneur must read about corporate or industrial history to glean the trends and know how the market has evolved, what's the burning issue to be solved and crystal-gaze into future to build a better and an impactful brand. Likewise, an author must read about the literary history to know what genres are most appealing to the readers globally and how the books of a particular genre have been treated historically. *Reading leads to better awareness. Through better awareness, we can make better choices and through better choices, however trivial, made everyday, we can be an asset to whichever team we belong.* While reading can be easy, making it a habit is what makes it stick forever. And this, perhaps, is the most common excuse we all give for not embracing good practices to fuel our growth. What if I told you there's a logical, scientific and yet a simpler way of dealing with it? Let's discover that up next.

45 THE TRILOGY OF '*HABIT-PASSION – WILLPOWER*' AND ITS LESSER KNOWN SECRETS

How often has it happened to most of us that we are desperate to start or pursue some new ritual or habit but it just doesn't kick off? And how often most of us blame it on time and circumstances? There is a simple but not often understood underlying cause for such kind of behaviour by most of us. Rather, I admit, any sane individual would do the same in almost all the circumstances barring exceptions when the stakes are high. The cause is simple – '**Lack of Passion**'. Lack of Willpower is only a manifestation of the same. To exemplify it, let's take it from where we left in previous chapter – *Reading*. Say, you desperately want to wire in a reading habit in your routine but aren't passionate about, you wouldn't even place an order on Amazon! or worse still, you would get one but it keeps lying on your book shelf for ages. Similarly, if you desperately want to get into shape and hence go for regular runs and workouts but aren't passionate about it, again you will often start finding alternate routines, say, going to the market even if it wasn't a pressing requirement thereby enabling you escape that activity while also giving you a valid excuse for your inability to do so. The English literature has coined a good term for it called '**Procrastination**'. A subtle way of saying *I will do it later (read Never)*. Before we dig deep, let's ask ourselves a fundamental question.

Is Passion in-born?

Once we realise the aforesaid cause(lack of passion), the next natural question all of us would pose would be this – Is Passion In-born? Does it mean that lack of passion will forever keep us from achieving such feats or installing such habits or routines? Obviously Not. But knowing just that doesn't suffice. It's important for us then to understand the mechanics of installing such routines. It all boils down to **a small but a miraculously impactful word – *'HABIT'*. Passion is all about doing what you like and liking what you do**. If exercising is your desire and not passion, it is going to be painful and thus you will keep hitting the market every single day! There is a simple, time tested and a scientifically proven way to defeat this *Self-Fulfilling Prophecy* which we all humans are so hardwired with – **Make it a Habit!** And once it becomes a habit, you will soon develop passion for it. In other words, passion is a natural fallout of habit. You can't be born with an inherent passion, can you? It's all about some trigger, some event, somewhere, at some point of time in our lives that we instantly get attached to and develop a deep liking for something. When aviators say, Flying is their Passion, I am sure they didn't cry for a fighter jet toy when they were infants but rather would have got a deep affinity to planes and jets by watching a movie or visiting such an installation or by seeing their own parents or relatives in such a profession. It's worth realising here, that quitting some bad habit or an addiction, say, alcohol, smoking or such other abusive practices also follows the same analogy and practice. Having been a chain smoker myself and having successfully broken out of its deadly shackles, I will walk you through how I dialled into the *'Habit of Not making it a Habit'*. But that's for another chapter to follow. For now, let's crack the code of Trilogy at hand.

The Habit Installation Mantra

Human minds are accustomed to instantly rejecting anything new especially if it endures some pain, effort or extra time. It might be surprising to note that there is a hormone or a chemical called **Cortisol** in our body that dictates much of this behaviour. Cortisol is a fear hormone that gets instantly released if you have been for long resisting something. And what's worse is, it only accumulates and multiplies over time. There is another culprit called **Dopamine** – A neurotransmitter or a chemical released in brain responsible for generating pleasure.

And pleasure, mind you is always derived from doing what you like and liking what you do. And again, like the former, Dopamine too keeps getting intense in quantity over time around a particular set of activities and thus keeps motivating you to continue doing stuff that you like – *binge watching movies or surfing on the internet for hours or consuming alcohol on a daily basis or smoking on an hourly basis.* All this just for one reason – We have defined our habits or fears which in turn drive these chemicals or hormones as a self defence mechanism. If a man can control a space ship in orbit, there is enough reason and resolve to believe we can doctor these chemicals too. And no rocket science or technical jargon involved to do that here! All we have to do is **divorce the *Cortisol* and befriend the Dopamine.** All you need to do is install a hardwired habit of doing it.

University of London has come up with a study that says it takes approximately 60 days to install a habit in your routine. A routine that will last a lifetime! And considering its longevity, 60 days shouldn't be costly, should it be?

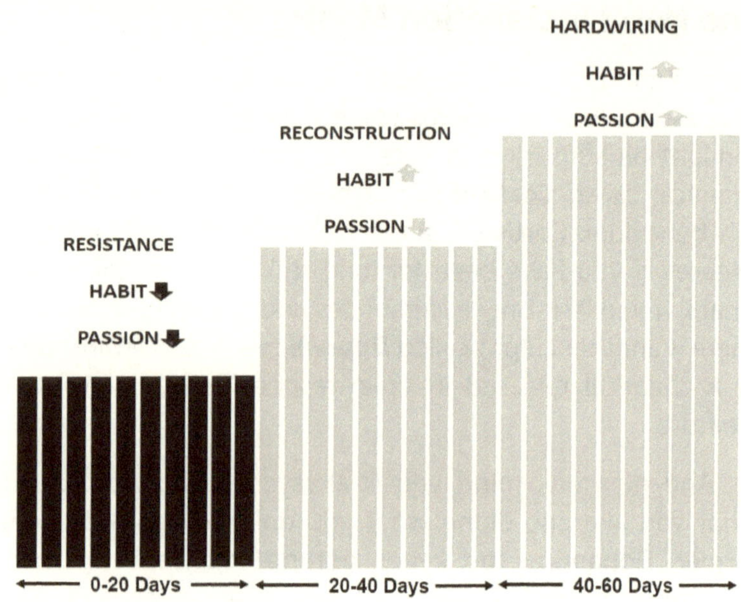

So far, we have come to terms with the analogy that you find it difficult to avoid procrastination if you aren't passionate about something and habit installation is a precursor to virtually inject the same. But, identifying WHY is only a part of the solution (albeit a major part). The tougher part is doing it. Though the university has laid down its own description of this process of habit installation, my personal deconstruction based on experience goes somewhat like this......

First 20 Days: Resistance

This is perhaps the toughest of all phases because you are challenging your normalcy and comfort zone! The only way to wither it out is *by just being at it*. '**Do it Anyway**' is perhaps one of the powerful phrases used by a renowned author and motivational speaker Shiv Khera as an explanation to his famous tagline – **Winners Don't do Different Things. They Do Things Differently**. Winners don't like to do things that are painful either. But they do it anyway and thus form the habit of doing things losers hate to do. It's as simple as that. Simple as it may seem, yet it involves some amount of tricking your brain. Some of the ways could be as given below :-

Trick your Brain by convincing that you are going to do the task for only a day. Then say the same thing to your subconscious mind every single day until you hit the 20th day mark. You will be amazed at how your body responds. I did the same during my quitting process of smoking. I just had to fool my brain that I won't smoke only for today. And it's seven years ever since. Phew! I am choicest betrayer, ain't I?

Evolve a self-reward system where in you promise yourself some reward (like a chocolate or an ice cream to eat or a movie to watch or any such amusement which is appealing enough) for successfully doing it for that day.

At the end of this phase, you would feel a lot different about yourself and guess what? the culprit *Cortisol* would now have significantly reduced.

20-40 Days: Reconstruction

If you have successfully hit this phase, kudos to you! This phase is a lot like the middle leg of a X-Country or BPET (Battle Physical Efficiency Test) route or a Marathon where in all you have to do is *Maintain your Pace*. **You brain starts reconstructing newer neural pathways around that particular habit you are trying to install** and soon you become more focussed and determined automatically to stick with it *anyhow*. And above all, your body (read mind) won't resist any longer; nor would you procrastinate doing that activity. At the end of this phase, you would have developed a strange affinity towards that activity and would even start having fun doing it. This is where you have begun to befriend your so-called pleasure reservoir *Dopamine* which was giving you pleasure for all wrong reasons. This phase by far is supposed to be the easiest phase to negotiate.

40-60 Days: Hardwiring

I use the term hardwiring for this phase because **hardwired beliefs, practices and rituals last a lifetime**. For instance, we are all hardwired to respect women and elders which becomes a non-negotiable mindset till our last breath. A much similar parallel can be drawn towards this phase. Halfway into this phase, you would already be finding it more difficult to not do the thing than doing it. This is where the process of hardwiring begins and soon it becomes a part of your daily routine and you would hardly feel worked up or committed in executing it. The day you hit the 60th day mark, you will really be proud of how far you have come and how capable you are.

Strange Phenomena of Willpower………

The best part of this whole concept of willpower is that you require it only for so long as you install a habit. Thereafter, it's kind of freed or released for many other rituals or habits to be installed. Take for instance, driving a car. I am sure all of us would have gathered significant amounts of willpower to learn driving but no longer require the same today as we simply walk out and steer away fearlessly! That's because, the reservoir of willpower is now freed and thus committed for some other pursuits and the chain goes on and on till eternity. **I can bet my last ten bucks on the fact that this mantra works miraculously well for quitting or overcoming an addiction to smoking or alcohol** (for that matter any such habit which is damaging your health).

Long and Short....

Our mind is an amazing machine if fed with the right inputs and rituals. **Habit, Passion and Willpower are so interrelated that they are kind of *Hand-in-Glove* and enable us humans to expand our comfort zones and lead**

a healthier and a joyful life. Just put the entire template explained above to any habit you have been longing to install (or de-install) but weren't just able to crack the code and unearth for yourselves the amazing results that will follow. **So, next time you hear someone saying 'I am passionate about XYZ', I am sure you will have enough reasons to believe you can develop them too!** Now it's time to reveal something very personal so as to help you all soar high and lead a happy and a healthy life. It's perhaps, one of the most productive chapters of this book. *Brace for Impact*!

46 SERENDIPITY FAVOURS OPEN MINDS

Call it adolescence craze or an addiction to venture out into unexplored territories in our teenage, most of us fall prey to some of the most damaging and soul crushing habits like alcohol, smoking and drugs. How I wish I was an exception. I was offered a cigarette at the age of 16 and I didn't blink an eye before grabbing it. You see, most teenagers suffer from the need of '**Acceptance**' and '**Fitting in**' and be the coolest guys/gals in the town. Thereafter, there was no looking back. I smoked my heart out like a chimney siphoning off about two packs a day (of 20 each). Yes, you read that right. I knew where I was heading (in fact, all smokers do) but just couldn't help myself.

Something strange happened in the year 2013 that recalibrated and reoriented my life permanently. During Golden Jubilee Celebrations of my unit, I was the LO (Liaison Officer) to our oldest commanding officer alive who was also invited. He was 77. That isn't being too old given today's average lifespan. But not if you are a smoker. As I went to visit him in his guest room, there sat a Military Oldie on the couch with a cigar in his hand and there began what would turn out to be my most life-defining conversation ever. I had heard of serendipity before but never really experienced it. It all meant hypothetical and theoretical to me. Not until I met this gentleman. The colonel was trembling to speak, shivering to the bones but yet gathered enough courage to take intermittent drags of the Vintage Cigar. There's something with these oldies and their proclivity with cigars, I tell you. Looking at me while he struggled to stay clean as the ashes soiled his attire like a child on a beach, he said *"Son, let me tell you something you may not know. Had I not latched on to this dirty habit of smoking, my life would have been a lot different today. I feel so helpless and defeated due to my ill-health inspite of all my achievements in the Military and shockingly I can't think of one good contribution this habit has had on my professional and personal growth. Don't ever pick it up"*

Those words kind of pierced through my body cells, let alone heart and mind. As shocking as it may seem, that was the last day I smoked. No rehab. No Nicotex and No gradual scaling down stuff that people recommend. That's what your own inner beliefs and faith can do. Talk about **Placebo Effect**! They say people do a lot for money, more for a leader but most for a belief. We all know how catastrophic tobacco is but yet most of us only have a superficial belief in it. Most of us are fence sitters, never realising when, on the slightest of trigger, we can easily jump over to the other side of fake-pleasure-seeking tobacco folks! For people who don't smoke or consume tobacco in any form (and hats-off to them for keeping that at bay), all this might seem *French*, but even as I write this, as per the recent survey by the WHO, about 22% of global population uses tobacco which includes 36% of all men and 8% of all women. Phew, that's a lot of human beings! According to the *Institute of Health Metrics and Evaluation Model of University of Washington*, an estimated 57% of world's population has been infected with COVID atleast once. It's a pandemic which, like Spanish flu, will fade away one day, albeit taking lot of lives. But what about the 22% tobacco consumption statistics which has been there for ages now and has taken many a life? Isn't it a bigger pandemic? This clearly explains why I say a strong and deeply ingrained belief is required to overcome any addiction. A belief which, in this case that *smoking is bad and will ruin your health and also of those around you* needs to get injected into your grey matter for only then will you be ever motivated to quit any harmful habit. A funny thing about any deep-rooted belief is that unless you proactively reinforce it, there is a great chance of it rising back to the surface and becoming a superficial belief, which soon evaporates. That's what happens to the so-called fence sitters which I referred to earlier. I have friends who quit smoking for five years, picked up again, smoked the heck out of their lungs, almost overcompensating for the cigarette-sabbatical, quit again for two years, began again, this time picking up a thinner one on the silly pretext of scaling it down and the loop never stops. I have stopped checking on their present status as it's futile. But I don't blame them for that's what any superficial belief about anything can do to you, let alone smoking. So, back to my story, knowing the power of deeper belief systems backed up by relentless reinforcement apparatus in our minds, I began my reinforcement process the moment I left from the colonel's room and how. Let's dissect any harmful habit and analyse how a person can be motivated to quit it. There are generally about four strong foundational reasons which propel you to quit and never start again. Smoking is my favourite case study as I have walked this talk, so let's apply this template to it.

How do you motivate a smoker to quit? Saying that *It Kills* isn't enough. It's as inadequate or insufficient as saying studying hard gets you good ranks and a job. You will still find children who hate to study. Hands on heart, having been there and done that, if you have never given a serious thought of quitting, the very thought scares you and gives you goosebumps. Let's walk you through the *Four Strong Reasons -*

On Health Grounds – It increases the chances of lung cancer by 80%. If this happens, which could and mostly does, you may not even be alive to see your hair grey and your grandkids blossom. Also, while you may live for about 70 years, atleast a decade into it would be painful and soul crushing both for you to undergo it and for your family to see you through it, it's as if you died at 60 but buried at 70!

On Family Grounds – Of all those who know you, it's parents and your life partner who will miss you the most after you're gone. More importantly, your partner because the kids will grow up or in many cases would have grown up already, to settle their own lives and he/she will most likely spend atleast a decade alone shuttling between children during festivities and otherwise. That's painful. And what caused it? Your obsession with tobacco which refused to stop entertaining you and you denied the thought of denying it.

On Financial Grounds – It digs a hole in your pocket whose size only grows with time while that of latter shrinks due to ever increasing professional and personal obligations. It's almost laughable because it's like spending money on something which attracts illness which in turn coerces you to invest a whole lot than you can ever imagine during the illness. Sadly, no money can buy a day's good health if the same money is used for decades to ruin it. As I write this today, given my strike rate,which I even used to foolishly boast about back then, I would have spent anywhere around Rupees 7 Lakhs had I not quit. For a humble middle-classer like me, that's a lot of money. That's serious

hard earned money. I may not have bought something substantial with that money but I bet I haven't spent much on my health issues either. It's square that way.

On Humanitarian Grounds – Your jaws will drop to know that passive smoking has equal probability, if not more, of attracting lung cancer. There are two kinds of second-hand smoke. Mainstream smoke that's breathed out by the smoker and side-stream smoke that emanates from the lit end of tobacco. Passive smoking can also lead to *Chronic Obstructive Pulmonary Disease (COPD)*, an advanced form of breathlessness or *Asthma*. Worst of all, pregnant ladies run the risk of *Low Birth Weight* and *Cot Death* in infants. Phew, so much so for professing kindness and humanity in today's world. You don't even need statistics to fathom it. Just look around your homes, colleges, universities and work places and you will know how many indulge in spreading passive smoke with friends who made the right choice not smoking but don't realise the horrors of the choice of having you around them or being around you.

Anyone or a combination of all of them can act as a catalyst to quit. What kept my belief reinforced was the second and the fourth reason. I knew I was a strong proponent of being a Good Human (or a Good Samaritan) and I loved my family more than anything else in the world (we all do). That's more or less what the rehabilitation centres attempt to do to your minds, subconsciously though. Since I did it consciously, fortunately I didn't need external help, except for that helpless yet humble Colonel who thought his noble words would be helpful in saving lives of many. And boy, did he save mine! You don't need a Rehabilitation centre. What you need is a Strong Belief which is reinforced by even Stronger reasons as above. Let me suggest to you with all humility, a simple methodology which I call '*Wrong Habits Annihilation Template*' (WHAT)

Wrong Habit(s)	**A *Belief* that most convincingly establishes that it's bad for you**	**Atleast 3 to 4 strong foundational reasons to *reinforce the belief***

Mind you, something as silly and simple as a *Bad Temper* or *Procrastination* or *Addiction to Social Media* is also a wrong habit. Mentally walk through the horrors or perils of not paying heed to those beliefs and reinforcing reasons. That, in the instant case study, might even amount to imagining your funeral with your better half and children crying profusely and refusing to let go off your body to be taken away to the cemetery. Reinforce that belief day in and out. You will be transformed. **While it may seem narcissistic or appear to be blowing my own trumpet, the point I am trying to make is simply this – Life is too short to experience it all yourself.**

So much so for beating a tangible addiction. The next chapter deals with an intangible addiction which few humans have managed to keep at bay!

47 THE MOTHER OF ALL ADDICTIONS

All through our lives at various stages (Childhood, teenage and adulthood), most fall prey to many addictions. Some latch on to smoking while few others get obsessed with alcohol. Many these days have even clung onto drugs falsely under the self-fulfilling prophecy of it being medicinal in value or claiming it to send you to seventh heaven. Some even are courageous enough to embrace all of them at once! Some other addictions include porn, food, caffeine or social media. But all these I must say are largely physical or tangible entities which we have attached ourselves to and which can be effectively combated through rehabilitations and counselling. *Yet, there is one addiction we are all born with; an addiction to which only self-realisation appears to be the antidote till date. It is an* **'Addiction to Instant Gratification'.**

Most of us need an immediate 'Well-Done' or 'Shabhash'(in Hindi) for every act of ours – Big or Small, Valuable or Invaluable, Consequential or Inconsequential. *We seek Medals and Certificates all the time till our last breath.* Aren't we cognitively imprisoned? We are too attached to incentives physically and emotionally which is what makes it more sensitive than all the other superficial addictions quoted above. I haven't heard of any rehabilitation centre to cure this because most of us don't even realise we suffer from it! And many others won't even accept this as an issue at all! So why is it dangerous? Let's explore….

While many might argue that this is the very basis of growth as it breeds healthy competition, I feel it's only partially true. The truth is that as we progress from education to jobs, *our own agenda undergoes a shift – a giant shift! which very few of us come to terms with.* **Our aspirations shift from being Self-Centric till the competitive entrance exams say medical, engineering, UPSC etc to being Team-Centric once we are enrolled**. Having said that, can a guy/gal still continue with the age-old rotten agenda of **Get-Get** even after getting a job? or should they now graduate to **Give-Give** of sorts and hence be more bothered of the overall well-being of the team? You have your answer, don't you? **This is precisely why you can bank on only a handful of folks when in trouble because all others are busy fulfilling their agenda of Get-Get!** Being addicted to gratification and incentive gets you so clung to the outcome that you almost forget the process which is more crucial. A more dangerous manifestation of this is the *'hook or crook'* attitude. The moment such people are denied incentives or a pat on their backs, their *shoulders droop and their energies sink in despair only to give rise to disgruntlement and crib!* Let Incentives be an effect of our deeds (and hence not sought) than a cause of our doings (and hence the primary goal). The joy of giving without expectations of return can't be explained in words.

Are you ready for a de-addiction? The Rehab Centre is located in your brain!

48 ANATOMY OF VICTIMHOOD

We all have come across people who have a zillion reasons on why something can't be done or achieved, often disregarding the very many ways of achieving the same. Even us (me included) would on many occasions have switched on the *Victim Mode* just to avoid something getting done. Of course, occasionally, that's understandable as you can't be on a *Full Throttle Msn Mode 24 x 7*. Our brains just aren't built that way. But what about those who are forever in the zone of playing victims? What about those who – unlike winners who have *Can Power* – possess a strong *Can't Power*? Let's dig deep into this kind of mindset to fathom the horrors of not shedding it right away to embrace the path of true self growth and development.

6 Jewels of Victimhood

A person who walks and talks like a victim will invariably embrace any or all of the undermentioned addictions which I call – because such folks really carry it like one and feel it hard to shed – as *6 Jewels of Victimhood*.

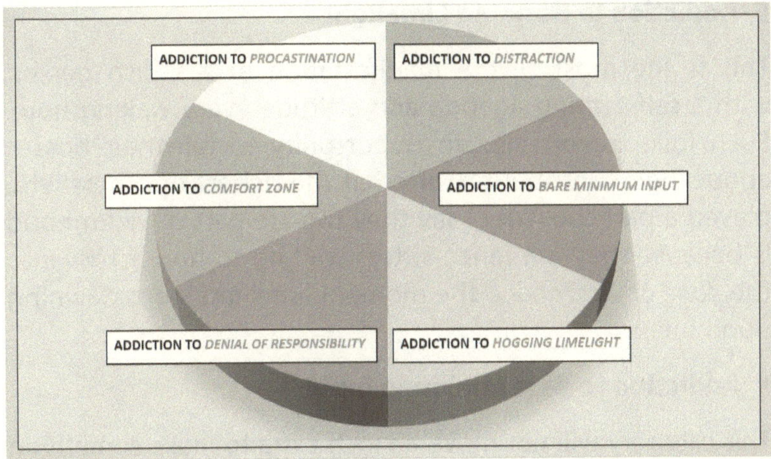

Addiction to Procrastination

This will forever they keep you from getting things done, howsoever big or small. In fact, the nature or enormity of a task isn't a concern at all. You are simply addicted to postponing things and since you need a cover up story for the delay, you start rationalising and reasoning, most of which are unreasonable and only reinforce the fact that you're behaving the victim way.

Addiction of Comfort Zone

This is the hallmark of all individuals who care two hoots about personal growth or impact. You will mostly be a passive passenger at whichever place you are planted. This clan has the most reasons for *Not Doing a Thing* as it contradicts their comfort zone theory.

Addiction to Denial of Responsibility

These people suffer from *Not My Job Syndrome,* often applying the template to their primary jobs, with strict boundaries about what's their mandated job. Such folks are harder to groom and nurture in your team because you need souls who go *Beyond Call of Duty* to make your team impactful.

Addiction to Hogging Limelight

This is the most severe manifestation of a selfish person with a self-serving agenda and attitude every waking hour. Such folks never miss an opportunity to tell their bosses about their contribution, often at the behest of others who played a part too. Why I say they too are part of victimhood is because they are fence-sitters waiting to hop across into the *Zone of Victimhood* the moment limelight stops dawning upon them.

Addiction to Bare Minimum Input

This category will not move an inch extra to make something better. In fact, contrary to their belief that they have done just about all it takes, they fall way short, many a times. In other words, they are capable of making a *Molehill out of a Mountain* and project it *exactly reverse* to their leaders. Imagine having 80% of your team operating in this zone!

Addiction to Distraction

This is more visceral & cognitive vis-à-vis others as it relates to 'Short Attention Spans'. You find it difficult to give singular undivided attention to the task at hand and are easily distracted by even the smallest of triggers like social media notification or random thoughts. As a result, both *Quality and Quantity* of your work gets affected and more importantly, you end up taking whole lot of time to complete even simpler tasks. And this applies to both professional and personal lives.

Mentally walk through how a person with any or all of these *Jewels of Addiction* would operate on professional & personal fronts and you will get a glimpse of victimhood. Corollary is pleasantry true. Go check out any individual who is highly impactful in your team or organisation – you will not find them embracing these addictions.

Self-Fulfilling Prophecy of Victims

Another appalling trait of victimhood is to blame it on *Luck* on failure & ride on *Efforts* on success of own and conveniently reverse this template onto others. Have a look at this template below:-

	REASONS OF OUTCOME	
	SUCCESS	**FAILURE**
SELF	**EFFORTS**	**LACK OF LUCK**
OTHERS	**LUCK**	**LACK OF EFFORTS**

Victimhood has all it takes to stall your growth & self-serve you to a fault. By merely shedding the aforesaid attitudes and prophecies, you can be a vital cog in the wheel on both professional and personal fronts.

49 TAKE TIME TO 'LICK YOUR WOUNDS'

> **"Only in retrospection will you appreciate God's reasons for the change in your circumstances and status. Don't deride him unknowingly".**
>
> **– Anonymous**

It's a common sight to see an animal licking its wounds in an attempt to self-heal the pain suffered. And if you have ever been vigilant enough, you would appreciate that they do it in an ultra-freakingly slow and deliberate manner. *There ain't any band-aid or medicine or magic pill (except of course for the privileged pets) but they are up and about in a jiffy leaving all the suffering behind, now treading more cautiously.* So much so for physical pain! I am sure they do self-healing of emotional pain as well. Isn't it an amazing attitude? They do teach us a very deep and a soul-searching lesson here and how!

Out of the total human beings alive on this planet, I wont be wrong when I say,99% have had some bad experience or an ordeal or are already undergoing a prolonged suffering and pain (physical and emotional). Rest 1% are lying! There isn't one person who can beat his chest hollow and declare that he or she is free of all problems or hasn't had an unpleasant experience in the past. *May I say with all humility that it's not the episodes of* *ordeal that define us but how you dealt with them and what hidden agenda of god could you glean and carry forward that does!* **Every bad experience is a Growth in a Wolf's Attire staring right at your face, point blank.** If you don't come out of your episodes with a fundamental change in your outlook, I dare say, you haven't learnt anything at all. While this may sound philosophical, my point is simply this – **Whether it's by the *Design of the Higher Powers* or by the *Default of Your Deeds*, every bad experience does sow a permanent seed of lesson in your gray mater.** *It's upto us to pause, retrospect, learn and rewire our methodology of how to play the 'Game of Life'.* They sometimes are simply designed to test whether you are a humble human who walks the talk or a hypocrite who only preaches and never does!

I am sure that every sportsman or a sporting team does retrospect deliberately after every loss. Why would you not apply the same to your lives? *The dictum of **'This too Shall Pass'** will only fructify when you let it pass but take the lesson forward lest God has, for reasons best known to him, unique ways of repeating such episodes or ordeals in multitude of forms over and over and over again.* As human beings and social animals, we all need both physical and emotional healing. Time does heal a lot but retrospection (read *licking your wounds*) will uproot your sufferings forever and grow you into a transformed human being.

Next time, you ever have such bad ordeals, do take time to Lick Your Wounds! Let me suggest a methodology to lick your wounds which can be maintained in your personal dairy as a reminder of how far you have come and how grateful you are to the circumstances that taught you a lesson or two. Pen down every single ordeal you have been through which was unforgettable and painful at the outset but ultimately fuelled your growth and realisation.

Ordeal (s)	What did it teach?	How much have you learnt on a scale of 0-9? (9 being highest)

50 ROLE-MODELLING IS A MYTH

We often hear people saying that XYZ is my role model. A cricket fan or in more generic terms, a sports enthusiast would say for example, Virat Kohli is his or her role model. Few others may choose, say, a celebrity actor like Amitabh Bachchan as their Role Model. The perspective that I am going to give you now might force you to rethink this whole gambit of Role Modelling.

Deconstruction of the term 'Role Model'

A role model is a person who you admire and whose habits, behaviour or demeanour inspire you to follow his or her footsteps in all walks of your life. It cuts across professions, geographical boundaries, ethnicity and gender. It was *Robert K Merton*, a prominent American sociologist, who first coined this term wherein he defines them to be reference groups who the people look up to or aspire to be.

Why Not?

There is no denying the fact that inspiration is more important than perspiration but here's a thing we must all ponder – Are these personalities the *Ideal Human Beings* on planet earth to emulate? May be not. In fact nobody is. Humanity is too complex a discipline for any single person to be an all-encompassing creature. Have you met someone who is quintessential testimony to every single good virtue of a good leader and a good human being? There's simply none in this world who can boast to have ticked all the boxes of virtues of being a perfect human being. Also, as most of us don't physically connect with these role models, does it even matter how many role models you have? The Singular Role Models have mastered a particular craft and to be a good human being (the single most important factor deciding how many will miss you when you're no more!), you need many other virtues too. Many, many of them!

You make someone a role model and soon enough he/she may end up doing something immoral. Your favourite actor might kill an innocent soul after drunk driving or slap an anchor on stage during Oscars; your favourite sportsperson may suddenly be caught doping or match-fixing or more popularly these days end up embroiled in *#Me Too Hysteria*. Your ideals then come crushing down like *jenga* and you no longer connect with that person and as a result, there is a big void in your inspirational bucket! Well, Good News. You can solve this dilemma by this simple technique.

An Imaginary Guru Does the Trick

What if you never had any such role model or Guru? How about picking and choosing a positive attribute or two from many, many of them and dumping it in an Imaginary Guru purely carved by your desires and limited only by your imagination. This guru will be tailor made for you, only you! That's when your life begins to dial into an upward trajectory setting lofty standards for yourself every waking hour, an ascendancy curve which may never dip. You could carve out an amalgam of 10,20,30 or even 100 individuals, who cares!

You see, if you are an aspiring cricketer, you would like to be batsman like Kohli, a strategist like Dhoni and a humble human at the same time like Dravid. Why, then, would you make anyone of them as your role model! You would rather have Koh-Dho-Dra as your imaginary guru, so to say. Likewise, an aspiring businessman would certainly want a patriot like Ratan Tata and a genius like Elon Musk both in one. As uniformed soldiers, we all aspire to be scholars, leaders and warriors together. Let me walk you through the following model which I call the **Imaginary Guru Inventory**. Write down every good virtue you want to imbibe in you as a leader and a human being and list out the individuals who you think are quintessential representations of the same. Your inventory is ready!

Virtues/Attributes	Name of the Person (could be your mom, wife, friend, celebrity, house help or any human being)

It's quite common for people to have mentors these days to elevate specific areas of their lives. Be it finances, health & fitness, spirituality, self-help & what have you! Yet most of it is premised on the concept of personal/group interaction either physically/digitally. In today's fast paced world punctuated by the ballooning social media, may I say with all humility that this may not be the most efficient way of self-growth. Consider this – Just by reading/watching about a personality & his/her work alone can inject an everlasting inspiration that guides us in our quest for self-improvement. And what's more, it doesn't have to be for a finite period because it isn't a course or a workshop. We are all works in progress & hence the workshop must continue till we kick-the-bucket! Does all of this require a physical/digital connect? You bet it doesn't.

If you have got my point, may I suggest a simple yet a powerful tool to keep your perspective aligned every waking hour. Place a board near your study table & populate it with photos of all humans (dead or alive) who have inspired you & about whom you have been reading or watching a lot lately. By merely staring at the board once or twice a day while you squat on your chair can alone be unimaginably transformative as they will act as an inspirational & a moral compass. *"You are the average of the five people you spend the most time with"* said Jim Rohn. I couldn't agree more.

51   LOVE YOUR *NAKED* SELF

Call it an obsession for physical fitness or a general dislike towards round and plum physique, I strongly believe that your physical appearance tells a lot about yourself. The depth and quality of love and respect you offer to those around you stems directly from the quality of self-love you nurture for yourself. Back in school days, my PT instructor used to say this while stressing on the importance of physical fitness – *"You must stand in front of the mirror naked everyday for 60 seconds and ask yourselves, am I proud of the way I look?"* We giggled it out back then being mischievous and kiddish. Strangely, it's all making sense some 20 years later and how!

So, what is it all about looking good? Is it your skin colour (which you inherited and hence have no control on) or your bearing and built (which you have 100% authority on)? No prizes for guessing. I firmly believe that our appearance is dictated by the two pillars of '**Diet'** and '**Physical Fitness**' and may I humbly suggest that the former's contribution is almost 80 %. *Abs are indeed made in Kitchen!* Let's deconstruct this age old conundrum of diet.

Building a Nutrition Narrative

I have yet to come across an overweight or an obese person who isn't a foodie! Of course, health issues like thyroid and many others which by design lead to gaining weight are an exception. And almost 90% of them blame it on **genetics** and **heredity**. *It's time we cut this **imaginary umbilical cord**.* What we eat is largely dictated by the *Nutrition Narrative* we feed our minds. If you are fat, blame it on this narrative which is driving your behaviour. And it takes courage to come to terms with this reality. Our narratives can be based on either of the two aspects – **Nutrition** or **Taste**. *Former propels your physical fitness while latter bloats your tummy*! It's fully conceivable that neither of them can be mutually exclusive but what's the larger proportion of it will dictate where we are heading. Consider this example – If you subconsciously feed your mind that *'xyz'* food (read junk) isn't good for your health and hence you hate it, you are more likely to come up trumps! Converse is uncomfortably true too!

There are countless number of good souls who are misled by their own narrative. A dear friend of mine who's battling the same says *'I want to enjoy life till 40 and will control my diet thereafter'*. Another friend said he *wants to quit military so he could eat well and savour all the goodies*! A classic example of how your own narrative can hijack your thoughts. You almost connect your concept of enjoyment to the food you consume.

Be a Poser Everyday

Ask any bodybuilder why do they pose so much in front of the mirror multiple times in a day and they will tell you. Pose in front of the mirror naked daily and ask yourself the same question – *Am I proud of the way I look?* I can bet my last ten bucks, it will begin redefining your narrative within a week! We will now analyse a closely related aspect of your appearance and find out how just one look at you can reflect a lot than you think to others.

52 YOUR PHYSIQUE REFLECTS YOUR *SELF-ESTEEM*

> **"A well-built physique is a status symbol that reflects your hardwork. Money can't buy it, nor can you inherit it. You can't steal it, nor can you borrow it. You can't hold onto it either without constant work. It shows patience, work ethic and passion. Being FIT is far more than just looks".**
>
> **– Anonymous**

I came across this interesting quote on the internet recently and it really intrigued me and set me into thinking *'Boy, I never thought it that way'.* Yet, there is a huge element of truth in it which cannot be overlooked. I feel it's more of a self-esteem issue here. Dictionary defines the phrase 'Self-Esteem' as a *good opinion of your own character and abilities.* In psychological parlance, it refers to *how much you appreciate and like yourself despite the circumstances.* More specifically, it simply means *'Self-Love'* (NOT to be confused with *Arrogance* and an *Inflated Ego*).

Having said that, one of the surest ways of reflecting your self-esteem (high or low) without even having to communicate is by means of your physical appearance. A well-built physique (NOT necessarily the six-pack-abs and shredded-cuts) reflects the depth of love you have for yourself amongst a whole bunch of other things or more holistically, it *reflects YOU just by one quick glance!*

> \# *It reflects the* **commitment** *you have to stay fit and healthy.*

> \# *It reflects the* **strength of willpower** *you have to exercise regularly and diet responsibly without making excuses.*

> \# *It reflects your* **priorities** *in life and hence your* **clarity of thought**.

> \# *It reflects whether or not you're a* **selective procrastinator** *and how much you love your* **comfort zone**.

> \# *More bluntly, it reflects whether you* **'Eat to Live'** *or* **'Live to Eat'**.

> \# *And finally, in more scientific terms, it reflects what gives you a greater* **'Dopamine-Rush'** *– 'A lavish Food' or a 'Sweaty Exercise'.*

It reflects your Self-Esteem .... All by Just **One Quick Glance**!

53 THE SOCIAL MEDIA ALA CARTE

> **"The internet is so big, so powerful and so pointless that for some people it is a complete substitute for life".**
>
> **– Andrew Brown**

In today's digital age wherein, we are at the cusp of turning every sci-fi movie into a reality, it's a no brainer to realise that unless we keep pace with it, we will be bypassed and turned redundant while those who cash on will reap fruits. Just like the Operating System of a smartphone or the smartphone itself, we will have to keep upgrading ourselves by learning (and unlearning) a universe of possibilities. One such universe is the Social Media. It's worth realising that with the ever-ballooning influence of **Internet** and **Social Media** on our lives, *never has it been so easy to make our lives marvellous and meaningful. There is nothing which Google can't search or YouTube can't play.* So enormous is its impact that many have even grown from rags to riches just by operating on this digital platter. Having said that, I dare say (and you wouldn't dare disagreeing either) that *it has also become doubly easy to fall prey to Negativity and make it a recipe of Duress and Disaster,* most often subconsciously, which is dangerous!

If we think it's the physical food that's keeping us healthy, we might want to have a look-see at *the content we are consuming digitally on a daily basis which is feeding our brains.* It's all about energies and we humans are *businessmen dealing in these energies – some productive* and some *counter-productive.* Let us see and realise how. Consider you have about ₹100 in a day which you have to intelligently invest in various portfolios to get maximum returns at the end of the day. What if you were foretold about a few of them that have always yielded losses? Would you still invest in them? I bet you wouldn't. Now *equate those ₹100 with the energy you have daily. Don't you want to invest this finite energy in something which gives you a positive return?* Yet, most of us fail miserably to understand it and more importantly refuse to accept it. We get hijacked by the **false pretext of being worldly wise by just indiscriminately grazing through everything on digital platform. It's time we customised our own platter! It's time we carefully chose from the Ala Carte of social media.**

An average Indian spends about **2.5 hours** on internet everyday. Let's ask ourselves a very harsh but a genuinely soul-searching question – ***What % of it do you devote to your personal and professional growth?*** Many would feel uncomfortable answering it! Blame the Platter that's feeding you and blame yourselves for not refusing to accept it. There's no denying the fact that some amount of entertainment is necessary for us humans but that shouldn't be all that you do feed on in a day!

I am sure watching a motivational speech by, say, APJ Abdul Kalam or Fd Marshal Sam Maneckshaw or Shiv Khera, reading about Mother Teresa or Malala Yusufzai or enrolling on an online course would leave you much energised, motivated and empowered at the end than watching and reading about the conspiracies surrounding a celebrity's suicide or watching the so-called Breaking News! Of the many disruptive technologies that have dawned upon us today, **Artificial Intelligence** or **Machine Learning** is, in my opinion, by far the most influential and impactful arsenal in the digital toolkit. You search something on Google and the algorithms fed to it are such that it's Ads and photos, related articles and such like posts that closely resemble the genre you searched flood your Google home page. Similar is the case with platforms such as YouTube, Facebook and Instagram. It's as if you went to a restaurant and enquired about the price of a Veg Margaretta Pizza and are soon presented with a buffet of 10 variants of it to choose from, often enticing you to buy more than what you can chew. And everytime you visit that restaurant, the waiter knows your taste and automatically lays out those varieties, this time adding a few more. The only difference, perhaps between the restaurant and Social Media is that in former case, you are actually presented with the product (or meal) which is prepared for you while in the latter case, you are the product. While Pizza might not harm you unless, of course, you have been binge eating, what you choose to consume on the internet has a profound influence in shaping your daily habits, routine and perceptions about this world. We need to ask a very genuinely soul searching question – *Are You Leveraging the Social Media or is it Leveraging You?* We will now see how counterintuitive is the real idea of social media and how is it coercing all of us into a trap. A trap called *Social Media Influencers.*

54 THE ABSURDITY OF 'SOCIAL MEDIA INFLUENCING' AND SKEWED METRICS

In the last decade or so, if there is one trend or practice that has sky-rocketed by leveraging Internet, it is this – **'Social Media Influencing'**. And sorry to dishearten the *Oldies*, it's as much common amongst them as it is amongst the *Millennials* who often get the notorious credit. And what decides how influential you are? The number of followers! How I wish this concept was genuinely true. Sadly, it's NOT. Infact, I am afraid, it never can be. Let me demystify this analogy. I have **two genuine arguments** with all humility to support my stance.

First, the literal meaning of *'Influence'* is **the power to affect or change somebody's behaviour or understanding**. Unless you are deeply touched or moved by a particular aspect of another person, you ain't **'Influenced'**. For all other instances, consider yourself to have only **'Interacted'** with these personalities (virtually or physically alike). Going by this logic then, hands on heart, *how many have actually influenced you till date? I am sure they are a handful and not a million!* This automatically leads me to my second argument – **The Skewed Metrics**. More the followers, more influential you are.

This generation (of course, how am I an exception!) is way too impatient with everything. Yes, everything – Be it career, relationships or any long-term pursuits. In short, my generation is by and large a clan of **'Quick-Fixers'**. Why wouldn't we be? Unlike 20th Century, we no longer must slog to start a business so that our off springs have a ball.

Lives today are transforming in a decade, forget about generations!

That very impatience has sadly coerced most of these 'Social Media Influencers' to resort to *getting a 'spike on their followers count'* because that's all that matters! Sure enough, they indulge in virtual barter – **You Follow me, I'll Follow you; You recommend me, I'll recommend you; worst of all, give me a 1000 followers, I'll give you a 1000 bucks**. I am trying hard to dig deep to fathom if at all there is some element of 'Influence' in all of this! While I couldn't find any of that, all I could realise is that it's all a *money minting game in the garb of 'Influence'*. That is not to say there aren't people who are genuinely influential. I do follow a handful of them who by virtue of their posts and comments, raise many a spirit and fuel my soul. Real Influence takes time and there's an element of *'Selfless Service'* in a *'Genuine Influence'* which automatically means you don't do it for *Money* as a primary aim but for the *Genuine Concern* . How I wish there as another metric added just adjacent to the followers button that read '**Deeply Touched**'.

Influence (if you must) your Kids, Parents, Partners, Peers and your *Spheres of Influence* at your work place We already saw what your sphere of influence can do in chapter 26. It may not be worth a million followers but definitely worth a million genuine good feelings and satisfaction for you would then have transformed lives of those around you.

55 YOU REFLECT YOUR COMPANY

> **"You are the average of the five people you spend the most time with".**
>
> **– Jim Rohn**

It's not uncommon for most of us being exhorted by our parents in our childhood to avoid *'Bad Company'*. They even went to the extent of asking us to befriend those who're academically sound and bright! While some might argue that this aspect of theirs was a bit *selfish and one dimensional* and not directed at the *wholesome development of their kids*, it mostly worked in our favour. *Extrapolate this concept to our adulthoods and make it multi-dimensional* (not just restricted to studies), a lot appears to make sense. There are two kinds of friends (read company). One that are **Valuable** and the other that are a **Nuisance**.

Valuable Friends are generally (and surprisingly so) less in number. They *add value to your lives by their mere presence and behaviour around you*. You share an achievement of yours with them, they will cheerfully open a bottle of scotch to celebrate out of genuine happiness. You share a failure or some bad experience, they will again cheerfully sit down for a comforting chat (even on phone) for hours like a *soothing emotional balm* and at the end of it all, manage to bring a smile on your face! You seek their help, and they go out-of-way to render help in any small way. Not an ounce of negative energy flows out of them and jealousy isn't in their dictionary. *You are energised after every single conversation, howsoever small with them.*

Nuisance Friends on the other hand, constantly drain your energy without even you realising it. You share an achievement, they are quick to share one of theirs without sparing a second to recognise yours. You share a failure or bad experience, they are quick to share one of theirs without sparing a second to pacify or comfort you. Worse still, if they don't have their own to share, they will share that of their friend's! but share they will. You seek their help, and they *go bonkers giving 100 excuses why they can't or hesitantly offer albeit with lot of emphasis on how they managed it!* And sure enough, *you feel drained after every conversation with them.* This might appear exaggerated but I hope you get my point.

It's entirely upon us to choose who we want to become and who we want to choose. Do you want to add **VALUE** or a **NUISANCE VALUE** to your friends?

56 WHAT DO MILITARY FOLKS AND ATHLETES TEACH US ABOUT STRESS MANAGEMENT?

Every human being on this planet has his own share of **stresses** and **anxieties**. The stress of *managing a job, a family* and *raising children* are necessary evils or **universal stresses**, so to speak, which every soul who is born has to go through in his/her life cycle. Yet, in my humble view, *a soldier and an athlete go through some **uncommon** and **extraordinary** stresses (in addition to the universal) which can hardly be felt through words*. Yet, I will attempt to briefly highlight the same to espouse my view to drive home a very simple, yet uncommon lesson to learn.

*A **Uniformed Soldier** (irrespective of ranks) withstands the stress of a harsh weather, a treacherous terrain, a determined and crooked enemy at the gates, many miscreants in the hinterland, occasional jolts of unfavourable govt policies and the heaviest of all – the burden of welfare of those under command and displaying quintessential courage and valour. The list is limitless....*

*On the other hand, an **Athlete** (NOT trying to strike any parallel but just one striking similarity), be it of any sport, combats the stress of remaining super-fit, fierce competition and* *criticism amidst media glare for poor performance disregarding the fact that he/she is just human. For instance, a 100 meters dasher practices for years to get a leap of 'One Second'. Phew!*

Yet, inspite of all these, they come up trumps every single time. Sure, the selection procedures in armed forces involves psychological filters and an athlete needs tons of will power. But they ain't super humans! They still knock down stresses and anxieties of all kinds with tremendous ease. Wondered how? While there are plenty of reasons in the list but this one certainly remains around the top – '**Sweat by Exercise**'. Yes, you read that right!

There is plenty of scientific evidence for the fact that a sweaty exercise promotes **Neurogenesis** – a process that grows newer neurons and repairs damaged ones. It's intriguing to know how! Our body contains a protein called BDNF (Brain Derived Neurotrophic Factor) or **Abrineurin** which is responsible for neurogenesis. *Every episode of stress or anxiety depletes it and hence your capacity to overcome stress. A sweaty exercise releases additional BDNF in our bodies which makes up for that loss and ta-da, you are game!* Not a single day passes without a sweaty workout for a soldier or an athlete and hence they are rejuvenated every single day. **If there's one habit we should all emulate from them, it is this!** Begin exercising. Today!

57 THE LESS EXPLORED PATH OF PROFESSIONAL NIRVANA

All of us humans are engaged in various jobs and professions today which are primarily based on the requirements of '**Earning Bread for Our Families**' and '**Making a Living**'. Few professions have '**Larger than Self**' causes like **Military** folks, **Astronauts** and such other disciplines where in your life is at stake every waking hour. Yet, irrespective of whichever profession we all are engaged in, there are two '*Underlying Aims*' with which we all walk up to our work places everyday. You can have either of them and **NOT** both.The two underlying aims are – aim to '***Do Justice to Your Position or Chair***' in your organisation or aim to '***Earn Accolades***' all the time from your bosses. Let's dissect the latter mindset first....

When you engage yourself with *'Earn the Accolades'* mindset, you subconsciously become very calculative in your approach. **Every action taken and word spoken will be calibrated with the thematic premise of securing your primary aim – earn praises and rise high**. You will constantly project your work, howsoever small, and look for small *'Bursts of Shabhash'* from your bosses all the time. Soon, the professional justice you ought to do to the position you hold takes a back seat and all your actions will be based on '***Work Where Visible***' theme which is dangerous. You will treat the present position as a stepping stone for higher positions because the concept of 'Win at all Costs' gets deep rooted in your gray matter. *The worst part of this mindset is that it constantly requires the Positive Feedback Loop of Praises to be completed for every action you do failing which you loose steam* *and feel disgruntled*. No surprises, your efficiency plummets manifold and you begin to feel unwanted or wronged by your organisation. You may not sleep every night with satisfaction and contentment as there is no end to human desires.

On the other hand, if your primary aim is to 'Justify Your Position', your energies and spirits are forever sky-high because earning accolades are never on your wishlist. I would be lying-through-my-teeth if I say praises don't make such people happier. Sure it does as we are *only humans* but it's just that *such folks don't expect it in the first place and consider any praises or a rise in hierarchy as a Bonus and a result of their deeds rather than making it the very reason of their deeds*. You will always see such people work as if their entire team's well-being depended on them and thus are adored by all and sundry. As they care two hoots about personal ascent up the hierarchy, they hit the bed every single day with tons of satisfaction and contentment. They, in other words, can be rightfully said to have attained ***Professional Nirvana'**. Go check out in any organisation, you will invariably find both kinds of people. **Are you courageous enough to take the less explored path? This less explored path, I tell you, is deserted and less crowded. What kind of human does it then turn you into when you embark on it? We will see that next.**

58 THE DESERTED ZONE OF NO COMPETITION

> "If a man is called to be a street sweeper, he should sweep streets even as Michelangelo painted or Beethoven composed music or Shakespeare wrote poetry. He should sweep streets so well that all the hosts of heaven and earth will pause and say, here lived a great street sweeper who did his job well".
>
> – Martin Luther King Jr

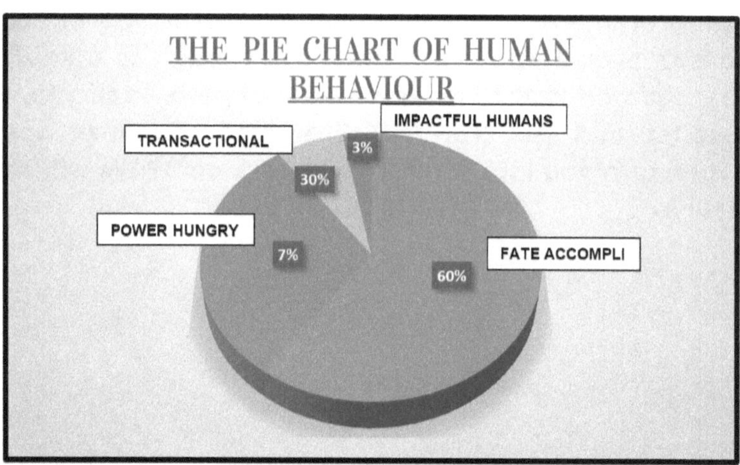

If you are heavily stressed in your lives, you may need to locate yourself in the pie-chart above and know why! The chart above shows 4 kinds of humans with their corresponding attitudes and behaviours.

Fate Accompli (60%) – They take it as their *fate to be just born as humans*, make peace with whatever they get by and *aim at making a living and no more*. Salary, Competence, Position and Fame are incidental. None will miss them if they dropped dead one fine day! Make their living a bit difficult and they will succumb.

Transactional (30%) – They *work their ass off their whole lives for a singular aim of getting good grades and a higher position* in hierarchy and no more. Salary, Competence, Fame and Living are all calibrated and intentional. They won't move a needle without a vested interest. Take off the incentive and they will become parasites. They are in essence *crooked* and base all their behaviours with an eye on the '*returns*'.

Power Hungry (7%) – Their sole aim is to become rich and famous with a whole bunch of working class enslaved to their whims and fancies. Salary, Competence, Position and Living are incidental. *Power is their oxygen and they would suffocate without it and would choke others with it.*

Impactful Humans (3%) – Their sole aim is to make a difference to the society and work place and in the bargain, inspire everyone around them. Salary, Fame, Position, Living and Competence are incidental. Nothing external to them at all, can shake them. They will be remembered for centuries, generations and ages.

I was fortunate to come across one such soul who I consider to be a quintessential example of Impactful Humans. Dedication, innovation and productivity are all proses of high end sophisticated desk jobs, they say. How I wish it were true. But it ain't because, I will tell you what a *Plumber* can do. Back in 2020, I was doing a year long professional course at Military Institute of Technology, Pune. For reasons beyond anybody's control, the size of quarters you got back then depended not on your seniority or rank but on the size of your family. There were 1 BHKs, 2 BHKs and 4 BHKs up for the grabs but with a catch. If you have a kid or two, you were easily eligible for 2 BHK or 4 BHK. But if you were a couple like me and my wife who chose to have a fun a bit longer before embracing parenthood, you were the chosen few invited to dwell in those match-box sized 1 BHKs. Things have changed, today, I am told, as everyone gets a minimum 2 BHK irrespective of his feeding strength. One fine day, one of the taps in our toilet gave in and suddenly decided to go berserk, leaking and sprinkling water all over the already sparse indoor space. It literally gave us a pre-shower before the actual shower next door. I requisitioned for a plumber on an emergency basis and the plumber arrived in 10 minutes. It was surreal for us to get such an instant response. But you will know why. His name was *Ganesh*. He came with all his arsenal which had tools that looked like fixing any plumbing issue on the planet, let alone a leaking tap. Little did I know that another morsel of serendipity was about to dawn upon me in next few minutes because what he did for next 60 odd minutes blew my mind. It will go down in my memory as the *greatest plumbing rectification* ever and the *greatest Impactful human ever*. It will blow your mind to know that too.

He examined the leaking tap which he fixed in about 10 minutes. Having arrived at 12 pm, he was free to leave by 12:10 pm but he didn't. He analysed the condition of the whole pipe leading to the tap outlet, declared that it's likely to give in too, in about a month and replaced the entire assembly with a brand-new pipe. He then looked at the knob of the flush tank and foresaw that it's nearing its shelf life and changed that too (apparently, I was about to tell that to him but in Army, you don't change something until it stops functioning). He gave me some math about a flush knob surviving some 600 push downs considering the daily usage rate which my mediocre mind could hardly fathom. But here was a man, who meant business and meant genuine service. It was now 12:30 pm. As he was about to leave, he suddenly found something wasn't right. He touched the walls of the toilet room which were apparently wet and told me it's unusual to which I gave an ignorant shrug. He then understood that there's some internal leakage of pipes beneath the walls which will not only waste lot of water but will also gradually weaken the wall which will eventually start caving in. He thus broke open the wall and reached the epicentre with surgical precision and repaired the leaking patch. At this point, though in lighter vein, I wanted to name him the *Plumbing Holmes*. But, boy, I almost bowed to him. He left at 1:15 pm, only to get back men to plaster it up in the evening at 6:00 pm. It took me a while for what had just happened to sink in. We aren't used to seeing that kind of dedication, are we? Are you? Sure enough, later, I learnt that he was the only one out of the three who was retained during COVID pandemic and the other two would never make their way back. So much so for productivity and desk jobs!

Long and short, if you belong (or decide to be part of) to those **sparse 3% of humanity**, *it doesn't matter which profession you belong to, you will be amazed at how little is the competition! Impactful humans always take the deserted route. Ganesh, a humble and impactful plumber, taught us that.*

59 THE PRIMAL FEAR OF ALL HUMANS

> "I just showed my plan to 1200 people. 900 said NO, 300 showed some interest, only 85 actually did anything. 35 of those were serious and 11 made me a millionaire".
>
> **– Bill Gates**

There is enough research and scientific evidence to prove that each human being's brain is uniquely built for revolutionising this world or more locally, our work places. It's just that only few are willing to harness that uniqueness into meaningful contribution in terms of innovations and creative ideas. Rest of the world is either *unwilling or unorganised* to make a start. However, there is another crucial aspect (read fear) which keeps our innovative minds at bay – **'The Fear of Rejection'**. This fear is ingrained in each one of us to varying degrees.

If we have been true to our jobs and been worth our salt, it won't be difficult to recollect numerous instances where in a bright idea or an innovation having the potential to transform your organisation would have stuck your mind only to find yourself putting it peacefully to sleep on the premise that it won't be accepted or worse still, that it might be ridiculed or laughed at! *We humans hate rejection!* Don't we? Haven't you stepped back from proposing to a girl fearing that it might be a 'NO' and hence settled for a *one-sided-admiration trip*? This isn't any different from the aforesaid analogy.

So, who's responsible for fixing it? Us or the Environment we work in? *I feel it's a bit of both who need an overhaul here and how!* Not only should we all develop enough courage to express our ideas without being worried of rejection, even the leaders at every level must also make equal amends to their work ethics so that everyone around feels secure to express and are fearless. *You see, there is a big difference in saying – 'That won't work or that's impractical' and in saying – 'That's a good idea, how about making these small little changes so that it all falls in place', when your subordinate walks up to you with an idea! The primal fear, hence, is to be overcome by both! Let's bite our tongues and accept the fact that, while the former fears rejection, the latter fears belittlement of his stature and maturity.*

So, next time something strikes your mind, remember, if you ask or say, the worst answer you could possibly get is a NO. But if you don't at all, the answer is already a NO. We will now see what happens when we push the fear way too much!

60 THE 'MR IDLI' SYNDROME

It's one thing to fear rejection and quite another to be careless about it. I would like to share a very funny experience which I had while driving down from *Pune* to *Bengaluru* with my wife and how even such simplest of incidents can sometimes convey a deep meaning.

As always, we were savouring the beauty of mother nature and the deserted road (courtesy the pandemic) which meandered through the hill ranges. As our caffeine addiction got the better of us, we decided to stop by for some coffee. As incidental as it may seem, we saw a huge hoarding onto our left which caught our eye! It read *Mr Idli Restaurant and Café*, 5 kms ahead. Besides rekindling my South Indian roots within, the name sounded interesting and we instantly decided it to be our halt for sipping some coffee. As we advanced, came another board which said 3 kms ahead, then another saying 2 kms ahead, then another every 500 meters. We gazed at each other and thought, Gosh! I guess we are in for some really reinvigorating café. Lo and behold, there came the café – It had just about 6 tables with 4 chairs each (even this is exaggeration) with its front board one-fourth the size of those hoardings enroute. How I wish I could take a picture of it! Are you kidding me? said my wife. *That really set me into thinking why did the guy blow his trumpet so loud when it had to turn out to be this? Why were his words roaring louder than his actions? What point is it at all to so fearlessly (read carelessly) announce yourself when there's no substance.* I guess it's the case with most of us today. Most people today work so little yet talk so much about it as if the world would stall if they stopped working! You will find such souls in every organisation without exceptions. ***We all suffer from this Mr Idli Syndrome to varying degrees***. And many don't even realise that they are subconsciously promoting and praising such individuals which is more contagious than even the deadliest of viruses! ***The irony is that, larger the team, less conspicuous it is.*** But it does have localised fractures in patches hampering the overall efficiency of the team, doesn't it? Consider an organisation or a company of 500 employees where in about 460 are *Mr Idlis*! It's more likely that the balance 40 will later, if not sooner, follow suit.

What the world needs today is **More Execution and Less Exaggeration**, **More Action and Less Words** or in hindi parlance **'Zyada Kaam aur Kam Zikar'**. What the world needs even more urgently today is *leaders who have the maturity to understand the difference between the two*. It's high time we eradicate the Mr Idli Syndrome.

61 YOU MANIFEST YOUR DEEPEST BELIEFS

> **"You are a living Magnet. What you attract into your life is in harmony with your dominant thoughts".**
>
> **– Brian Tracy**

We have often heard of the phrase '**Shub-Shub-Bolo**' from our forefathers, friends and well-wishers. While that could well have been out of genuine concern for our well-being, I have a strong feeling that in many ways it's spot-on when it comes to manifesting your life, surroundings and future.

I am tempted to share a small story of a certain Hal Elrod of California, USA who for me, is the quintessential testimony of how beliefs manifest our lives. At the age of 20 when our teenage blossom is in full-throttle, he met with a deadly car accident (hit by a drunk truck driver) which split his car into two and arrested his heartbeat for six long minutes with a dozen broken bones. This left him comatose for weeks. He survived. As survival was itself a boon, he was declared paralysed for life by doctors and most likely would have to spend his entire life on a wheel chair. But, he recovered and not only walked but also ran Ultramarathon much to the shock of all his doctors. Just as he thought his life was back to normal, he was diagnosed with a rare cancer followed by multiple-organ-failure which began shutting down like streetlights in a metro city hit by a power outage. He survived again! Not surprising at all that today, he has written a few books including the blockbuster 'The

Miracle Morning' and is also a keynote speaker at various cognitive domain related workshops, schools and colleges. As he shares in one of his interviews (and of course in his book too), Not for once did he think of dying after the accident or during his bed-ridden ordeal at the hospital. Not for once did he think of succumbing to cancer and the painful chemotherapy. His entire body, mind and soul was devoted towards recovery that included visualising himself 'running' after recovery and helping people globally realise the power of belief (read positive belief). And guess what, he is doing exactly that today!

Our mind is a miraculous and a complicated arsenal which very few have mastered the art of nurturing. It manifests whatever you feed it. Read that again! Consider these simple instances -

> \# If you have a sore-throat and you start fearing about COVID day in and out, you will most likely get infected with it. **Thanks to you!**

> \# If you have an occasional chest pain and you start fearing a cardiac arrest, your mind will manifest it someday. **Thanks to you!**

> \# If you walk into a game thinking how to avoid defeat rather than how to win, you will most likely lose. **Thanks to you!**

> \# More generally (and we have been fed with this narrative since our childhood), If you think you Can't, most likely you won't. **Thanks again to you!**

I would be lying-through-my-teeth if I say believing in positive outcomes always and everytime is the easiest thing to do. It sure isn't. But pessimism is yet to favour any human on this planet till date. Some research says an average human gets about 46000 thoughts a day. But it's not the quantity but the quality that matters. Your deepest beliefs are your strongest foundations and that's what will exactly manifest.

62 THERE ARE NO INTROVERTS ON THIS PLANET

Most of us are quick to declare a person an *'Introvert'* just by virtue of his/her social conduct. Being vocal is so very attached to the term 'Extrovert' today. However, we also collectively agree that a person needs to have *'Good Communication Skills'* to be an effective and inspirational leader which automatically means being an *'Extrovert'*. Ironically, how are then some of these Introverts great leaders in many domains? You just need to check on the internet for the names that can put you in a fix! Isn't being an *'Introvert Inspirer* or *Leader',* an oxymoron? It's high time we shed this false narrative and redefine the term.

In today's age of *influential social media* coupled with age old *'FOMO'* syndrome that refuses to part with us humans, I dare say, *it's almost impossible to stay Introvert even if you are least social.* A careful dissection of the term would reveal an interesting manifestation of this trait through the following analogy.............

In a normal social gathering, you will normally see extroverts making announcements or declarations much in a desire to be the centre stage of any large group conversations. Whereas an introvert can be seen engaging in individual conversations rather peacefully with the sole aim of making the event memorable through richer conversations. Thus, Introverts today are Selectively *Extroverts.*

It's foolhardy even to compare the two traits and conclude which of the two is better as long as our behaviours lighten up the mood of others and inspires them. We have a choice to be Extroverts or Selective Extroverts and both are absolutely OK !

Not all extroverts are revered, are they? A careful dissection of the *'Extroverts'* clan will reveal two broad categories – **'Knowledge-Centred'** and **'Self-Centred'**

Knowledge-Centred – These individuals, though always engaged in a monologue in any gathering, do so with a genuine intent and desire of sharing some piece of information or knowledge which the feel is worthy of spreading. Sure, they end up over-doing it quite often, but the audience can bear it as deep down, they do know that their awareness is being enriched.

Self-Centred – These individuals are *'painful'* as they engage in self-centred talk sharing their achievements, memories, likes and dislikes little realising that nobody GAF about it. Yet, they keep sharing and sure enough, the audience can't bear it as deep down, they do know that their precious time is being mercilessly slaughtered!

Given a choice, I would love to be a Selective Extrovert or a Knowledge centred Extrovert.

63 DON'T JUMP THE QUEUE

It's one thing to be fearless about death and quite another to have the desire to live long. **Yet, a person who has this duality isn't a hypocrite**. Lest the entire fraternity of armed forces would be labelled as such because they signed up as they didn't fear death but would want to serve for as long as possible. *If a person fears death, it automatically means he desires to breathe till eternity for reasons best known to him/her. On the other hand, if a person isn't afraid of death but desires to live long, it's reasons are best known to all and sundry – to have an impact on this world by inspiring and uplifting humanity through sincere service for as long as possible.*

Ever since we all were born, we were mustered automatically along a 'Queue' to the ultimate climax – the Death. And as long as you don't jump the queue, you will '*Kick the Bucket*' only when it's your natural turn or in other words, when you are destined to. Yet, so many of us are so embroiled in chasing multitude of desires in the garb of 'Getting Ahead in Life' that we subconsciously '*Jump* the Queue' – read that again and let it sink in!

Answer these simple soul cleansing (yet crushing for few) questions to yourselves –

Aren't you jumping the queue when you overspeed on a highway?

Aren't you jumping the queue when you get ferociously addicted to alcohol, tobacco and other drugs of fake joy?

Aren't you jumping the queue when you disregard the health advisories during a pandemic?

Aren't you jumping the queue when you are consistent as hell in consuming unhealthy food or are even overeating healthy food and are growing obese?

Aren't you jumping the queue when you don't exercise daily in the garb of being 'busy'?

Aren't you jumping the queue when you are emotionally hurt due to family woes and you don't commit to resolve it? (Emotional health has far reaching effects on longevity than physical health).

Aren't you jumping the queue when you needlessly and endlessly work your ass off disrupting your daily routine (including sleep and food) just to prove that 'You are the Best' to your boss who couldn't care less?

Perhaps, this is the one and only queue in our lives wherein we aren't objected to when we 'Jump' because very few are in a hurry. If your answers to the aforementioned questions are a 'YES', I am glad you got my point. Every action of ours must invariably be premised on these questions. Because, every humble human being alive on this planet has a longing desire to have a happy family, see their kids grow and perhaps even their grandkids grow and in the process, be as ideal and inspirational role models to them and the outside world as possible. Yet, many are impatiently jumping the queue. According to Dr David Sinclair, a renowned scientist and an author, considering the advancement in health sciences, humans who will push the brink of 120 years of age and reach even upto 150 years are already born. They will succeed eventually in making that a norm, he says. But not if they too are jumping the queue!

If You really want to make a difference or an impact and leave a legacy behind, '**Don't Jump the Queue'**. Take a Giant Leap instead towards *Championhood. And that's where we will dive into the penultimate chapter of our journey together.*

64   TAKE THE GIANT LEAP

> "I am NOT what happened to me. I am what I CHOOSE to become".
>
> **– Anonymous**

We all humans across the globe have an innate **'Narcissism'** that resides within. It only manifests to varying degrees in our behaviours based on how we have trained our minds. Surprisingly, little do we realise that this tendency of **'Self-Importance'** leads to a sense of **'I am OK, World is not OK'** mentality that seeps into our grey matter which soon turns us into a *'Victim'* and how!

Take this instance. We all confront numerous situations or problems each day both on professional and personal fronts. A little retrospection of how most of us deal with them daily would reveal that each time we are confronted with a problem or an issue, our immediate and natural reflex is to blame the environment. We resort to this so as to preserve the same **Self-Fulfilling Prophecy** of 'I am OK, World is not OK' and thereby pass the buck to external conditions (people and environment). This leads to a subconscious addiction to **blame-game**, a defining trait of **Victimhood** and that's self-defeating in the long run. Imagine the plight of a company of, say, 50 employees in which everyone has this innate narcissism!

It's worth realising that irrespective of the nature and degree of problems we confront, there are very few in which we ourselves have absolutely no role to play in their development. If you are courageous or willing enough to come to terms with it, may I suggest to you, with all love and respect, a simple exercise or experiment.

Note down atleast 5 issues or problems that are plaguing your mental peace for long. Deconstruct each of these from the point of conception till its final development today. You will be surprised to realise that most of them (if NOT all) would have some contribution from your side – be it your response or behaviour or conduct which ultimately led to its present day irritable form. By doing this, you are re-wiring your brain away from Victimhood and aligning it with **Championhood***. You will now subconsciously stop playing blame-game and start focussing on how you can handle the situation better so that your contribution is ZERO in it.*

And no surprises, as you cancel out all those issues for which you are a partner in crime, there will hardly be any left which is pleasantly comforting! You then wake up to the fact that **by changing what's within, you can change most of what's outside**. Subconsciously though, a narrative of **I am OK, World is OK** gets fed into your mind and soon enough, you will be a transformed. In other words, you take *the Giant Leap – A leap from* **Victim** *to* **Victor;** A leap into a territory where very few reside and are hence the world-changers. Too very few are willing to take this Giant Leap. Are You?

65 THE 24 KARAT HUNT

"Everyone of us is a perfect human being deformed by the family, society and the culture".

– Alejandro Jodorowsky

We are expecting our first child in September 2022. It's such a blessing and a god-sent gift to be able to raise a raw and brand new human being who is waiting anxiously for nine months to explore this world and contribute to humankind through the guiding light of parents. As future parents, I often ponder with my wife Kritika as to how we must give the best environment to our child for its growth and development while we ourselves carefully conduct to be the best role models a child can ever dream of. As a write this final chapter in my study room with a cup of soul-soothing coffee post our routine visit to Hospital, it's almost as if my whole of upbringing and value system is acting as an invisible force behind to enable me pen down my authentic and true wishes as a humble and responsible citizen of this planet.

Think about this – *A parent sacrifices a whole lot than you could possibly imagine to ensure a good education and upbringing of the child. It's only fair for them to expect their children to be happy and successful. A child on the other hand, who came into this world only on its parents' desire, does his/ her best to make parents proud and make an impact. It's only fair for children to expect parents to be considerate when their aspirations don't coincide or when the child stumbles occasionally. A teacher (worth his/her salt) goes full throttle in making efforts to impart knowledge to the students. It's only fair for them to expect their students excel in life. On the other hand, a humble and hardworking student is always willing to learn and go to any lengths to readily imbibe what's being taught by the teacher. It's only fair for them to expect the teachers to understand their needs and capacities and make amends. A soldier in the military puts his life at stake every waking hour (and even while asleep) to safeguard the territorial integrity of the nation within whose borders, you and me sitting in air-conditioned rooms from afar can tweet and re-tweet about the efficacies of 'Agnipath Scheme' or 'OROP'. It's only fair for a soldier to expect his government to take good care of his family when he's no longer alive. A military veteran would have spent about 50% of his adulthood in serving the nation, walking on a tight rope overseen closely by an even tighter scrutiny of his conduct under Army Act depriving few of the fundamental rights enjoyed by you and me. It's only fair for him to expect his government to pay heed to his aspirations post retirement. Let's go macro now – A honest tax paying citizen wouldn't move a brick if it contradicts the value system of a Good Citizen enshrined in the Constitution. It's only fair for him to expect his political masters to look after him and his aspirations rather than looking after their own luxuries and privileges. Going very generic now to drive home a point – A honest, humble, dependable and hardworking employee of any organisation would go an extra mile, every single time, to ensure that the desired impact is palpable and eventually help the organisation soar sky-high. It's only fair for him/her to expect the bosses and management to be empathetic to his/her needs and aspirations and above all, expect an environment conducive to growth, happiness and satisfaction.* While all these expectations are fair and square, what are we all saying in unsaid words? We want this world to be *Ideal* and *Perfect*. And mind you, the definition of idealism is unique to every single human being who's alive and kicking on this planet. In other words, we want everything and everyone around us to be in their most authentic and purest form, devoid of any harmful and ulterior motives – **As pure as 24 Karat Gold!** So much so for expecting or receiving from outside. But what about giving? *"Only by giving are you able to receive more than you already have"*, said Jim Rohn. While we expect all and sundry to be 24 Karat, the first step towards ushering the same into our lives is to be a 24 Karat ourselves. No matter which family or background or community or religion or country you are born in, you invariably perform these eight roles – *A Child, A Parent, A Teacher, A Student, A Leader, A Husband/Wife/partner, A Subordinate and A Citizen.* We are 24 Karat when we are born as I said this earlier in the chapter on *'Why Restore'* and are only seduced into the hypnotic practicality of society and culture. I know it sounds philosophical but allow me to emphasise – If everyone did his job to the best of his/her abilities with a sincere intent of service, imagine how blissful, charming, encouraging, inspirational and wonderful your family, organisation, country and world at large can turn out to be. What if every leader leads like he's the best in the world and of course, has the best team in the world? What if every employee/subordinate works as if they have the best leader and team they could ever dream of? What if every parent and child conduct as if they are the blueprint of a happy family? What if a couple live and love as if they are one soul in two bodies? Above all, what if every human being strives to be 24 Karat in every role that he/she plays? Let me ask you two simple questions – *How difficult it is for you to be one like that? And Don't you think, even if we don't achieve a 100% transformation, world would have still gone many many miles far towards making every home, workplace and the planet at large, a wonderful place to reside?* It's disheartening to see many people detesting the *Idea of Idealism* on the pretext that *Nobody is and can be Perfect* and hence using it as a sledgehammer of eroding values and an anvil of harbouring *Practical, Profitable* and *Self-Serving* attitude. You may never reach 24 Karat. But what good is it to be a10 karat on that premise? Will you be as impactful? We are all *Works in Progress*. The progress is faster if the work is harder but work we must, to be the *Best Versions of Ourselves*; to be our own versions of 24 Karats – authentic and devoid of any adulterations. As we now draw close to end of our journey together, before you lay the book to rest, may I suggest one last exercise to keep our perspectives in good health. Make a list of attributes of an Ideal Daughter/Son, Son-in-Law/Daughter-in-Law, Father/Mother, Teacher/Student, Leader/Subordinate, Husband/Wife/Partner. See how many of the boxes of these attributes do you *tick* and you will know where you stand and where can you do better by disregarding the mythical lies our culture and society sells you. Only then, will you be called (and don't you want to be remembered as?) – **What a Gem of a Soul!**